WOMEN AFTER PRISON

Mary Eaton

OPEN UNIVERSITY PRESS
Buckingham • Philadelphia

Open University Press
Celtic Court
22 Ballmoor
Buckingham
MK18 1XW

and
1900 Frost Road, Suite 101
Bristol, PA 19007, USA

First Published 1993

A catalogue record of this book is available
from the British Library

Library of Congress Cataloging-in-Publication Data

Eaton, Mary.
    Women after prison / Mary Eaton.
        p.   cm.
    Includes bibliographical references and index.
    ISBN 0–335–19008–1.   —   ISBN 0–335–19007–3 (ppk.)
    1. Women ex-convicts—England—Case studies.   I. Title.
HV9649.E5E28   1992
364.8'082—dc20   92–14875
                                                            CIP

Typeset by Inforum, Rowlands Castle, Hants
Printed by Great Britain by J.W. Arrowsmith Ltd, Bristol

CONTENTS

ACKNOWLEDGEMENTS

This book would not have been possible without the assistance and co-operation of a number of individuals and institutions.

First of all, I would like to thank the 34 women who gave me their time, their trust and their life histories. By their courage, perseverance and good humour in the face of extraordinary difficulties, they also gave me hope.

The award of the Morris Ginsberg Fellowship, from the London School of Economics and Political Science, made it possible for me to be released from teaching duties to do the research. A grant from the Nuffield Foundation paid for the transcription of the tapes on to disk. St Mary's College, Strawberry Hill, gave me six months' leave. Colleagues and students there continue to make it a stimulating place in which to work.

Throughout the time in which I was engaged on this work I received help, advice, and frequently much kindness, from the following: John Adams, Eileen Boothroyd, Julia Brophy, Joan Cauldwell, David Evans, Patricia Gracey, Olga Heaven, Frances Heidensohn, Mary-Jo Hickman, Jean Howard, Derek Julian, Jackie Lowthian, Jill Matthews, Jennifer McCabe, Sue McDougal, Roberta Meredith, Terence Morris, Helen Taylor, Alison Trundell, Antonia Watson and Celia Willoughby.

Julie Smalls cheerfully and efficiently transcribed the data and processed the words, and did much more besides.

I owe a very particular debt of gratitude to Pat Carlen who provided encouragement, cogent criticism and wise counsel, at every stage of the work.

Chris Tchaikovsky made so much possible. Through her good offices I gained access to people, places and perspectives which would otherwise have remained inaccessible. She gave freely of her time, her attention and her considerable expertise. Her enthusiasm for the project was inspiring and her critique invaluable.

1

YOU CAN'T PICK
AND CHOOSE

In January 1991 Alice was 24 years old. She had served three prison sentences, all for deception. This is her story.

My mum left me and my brother when I was five and she went off with someone else. My dad got a woman to look after us. She abused us and somehow the social services got to know about it, and we were put into care. About five months later they asked us if we wanted to go back, and I did. I never thought about all the bad things that would happen. Home was a mum and a dad. But my brother he was older than me, and maybe a bit wiser, he refused to go back. And things were worse, much, much, worse.

Eventually when I was ten I got the courage to run away. I tried to tell the headmistress what was happening but things like that didn't go on in those days – really she made me feel more guilty than anything. She stripped all my clothes off me and looked for marks on my body and I don't think she believed what I was saying. She called my stepmother up to the school and my stepmother used to have to visit every Friday after that. I think it made it worse in fact. School was an escape, so, I suppose my behaviour was a bit weird but it wasn't bad. In fact she told me to be bad, so when she used to come to the school and hear that I wasn't being bad, or whatever, I was in trouble with her – she just wanted me to be a bad child all round – she just controlled me, told me what to do. I had no choice. My dad was never there and he didn't seem to like me much anyway. So I got the courage to run away.

I ran away to my friend's house and contacted the social services. I thought my life was at risk and I didn't want them to tell her where I was. I didn't even want to tell them. Eventually it all came down to the fact that they said to me 'You can't pick and choose where you want to go. You've got to go to foster parents'. So I went to foster parents and that didn't work out. Then my stepmother left my father and my father mentioned to me that he wanted me to go and live with him. I think he was just saying it out of being fatherly but I took it that he was being serious: 'Oh that'd be great Dad!' Just me and my dad. So I ran away from my foster parents. I went to live with my dad. And again they said to me 'You can't pick and choose where you want to go'. And they put me back in a home.

A couple of months later my dad came to pick me up and he had another girlfriend who had two of her own children. I went to live with them and it didn't work out. It wasn't my family – his girlfriend, her children – and all my thoughts and feelings were mixed up – what I was feeling inside – I couldn't cope. And I used to stay out all night and go here and there, and swear and be bad and everything. And one day my dad, as far as I'm concerned if I hadn't stopped him he would have tried to have sex with me. So around this time my mother was back on the scene. She had some shops and we were driving through this town and my dad said 'Oh there's your mum's shop'. And I said, 'Oh my mum?' I couldn't believe it and I was just adamant then that he should take me to see her and he did and that's how we got back in contact.

She phoned and she asked me to go and stay with her and I told her what happened with my dad. And she said, 'You're not going back'. And I didn't want to live with her, I had no choice. People came, I made a statement. This is when I was 12. I didn't know they were charging my dad, I didn't know, I didn't know what was going on. No one told me. I just done the usual – my life just lived – I didn't fight or talk or anything I just used to have bad behaviour – funny behaviour. I ran away from my mum's – I was about 15, something like that, and it just totally didn't work out. And I kept running away, running away. One day when I ran away the police picked me up and they said 'Your mum has decided that she can't take you back any more'. So they put me in the cell and this man came to pick me up, then I went into an assessment centre and from there I progressed to what's called a woman's hostel which is like an older version of a children's home where they teach you to look after yourself before you leave.

I was 18 when I left care and was put into a flat. I couldn't cope. I started with a certain crowd of people. I met this man who I became infatuated with. I was working when I left care. I resigned because I couldn't cope with all the feelings I had inside. I didn't know who to talk to or how to deal with it. I was in this flat, I met this man. He was into all sorts of things but that didn't have any effect on me. Because of the upbringing I had I wasn't choosy, I was pretty naive anyway. And because he was seven years older than me I thought he was mature. I realize now that I was an easy target because he realized that I had my own bank account, my own Access card because I was working. And he never forced me to do anything but he more or less said 'Oh you can do this' and 'Come on let's go and do it'. And I never really spoke up for myself, I didn't speak up, I just went and done it, having faith in him that he would protect me and whatever and having faith in what he was saying. Although I knew it was wrong I didn't know how wrong – it's confused.

The first thing I ever done was instant credit – telly and a video or something like that – and then it progressed from there. I got away with quite a lot with my own cheque book and card – or I'd go to Marks and Spencers and you can write cheques for large amounts and take back the clothes and re-fund them. That's how I eventually got caught because when I went back to get a refund they had someone following me from Marks and Spencers. They then followed me to Dixons where I was trying to deal with the credit and then they called the police.

I was put on bail straight away – no previous at all – then I started on stolen cheque books and cards. I was arrested again and papers were put together and it all amounted to about eighteen thousand pounds – something like that, a lot of money, that they could not get back – maybe that's why I got

such a hefty sentence. But the second time I was arrested I
was refused bail totally and when I finally went to Crown
Court I'd done five months and I suppose they thought,
'Well, might as well round it off – 9 months' – and I was sent
to – back to Holloway and I went on to Bullwood Hall where
I finished all my sentence. And I came out. I went back to the
same man, basically because I didn't know there was anything else I could do. I didn't think about anything else. I
thought I loved him. I think I did. He was a violent man. I
think that's why I couldn't really leave him. He was violent
and I had a determination to stand by him and prove to him
that I was worthwhile, that I wasn't the woman he said I was.
He accused me of going about with other men and all that
sort of thing.

When I came out I didn't want to do it again, but we had a
mortgage on a house and when I came out he was in a terrible
state – he'd sold everything that we'd had, even my hairdryer.
There was just nothing in the house at all. And the night I got
out he didn't have any money. He asked how much money I
had on me – they give you like a payment when you leave
prison – he took that – he used to gamble a bit on fruit ma-
chines – and then he produced the cheque book and he said to
me 'Do you want to go and get us something to eat from the
Indian?' And I said to him 'No', but then I was afraid because
he was all I had and I was just – I realized that we would either
starve or – you know – it was just a confusion.

I did try with my mum but she didn't want to know. This
man used to attack me and kick me – I used to manage to get
away. I know I used to always go back but I believed that he
loved me. I wanted so much to believe that he'd be different
and that my coming back would prove to him that I believed
him – and he was telling me that he'd changed and everything
and everything'd be changed and he'd believe I don't want
any other man. I love him and I want our home and his
children and whatever. And it never worked out that way.

He was just really terrible – the few months I was out was
virtually hell really and I went into a battered wives' home as
well and I was taking drugs. I never got addicted to anything
but I was just living a whirlwind of a life – crime and going to
clubs – all over the night – taking drugs. I didn't stop to think
'What am I doing?' I just did it. I ended up back in prison
again.

During her prison sentences Alice had sought help for her feelings. She saw a psychiatrist in Holloway:

> The man was shifting in his chair. He didn't have time and he must have thought 'Oh God, another sob story trying to get off her case', but it wasn't. I was trying to tell him how I was feeling – the pain I was feeling, and the confusion and he just wasn't interested.

In Bullwood Hall, her experience was similar:

> I saw the psychiatrist and he was so busy just staring out the window and all he wanted to do was put me on medication and I don't believe in medication, taking drugs and everything, if I want to get high or whatever, but not when you've something serious like that. It would have been very easy to be like some of the other girls and escape with drugs. But I had a strength that I just refused to be drugged and I said 'I don't want drugs – don't you understand what I'm saying to you? I have a serious problem'. And I never saw him again.

During her second prison sentence Alice lost remission and gained a reputation as a difficult prisoner.

> A group of us kicked our doors because they wouldn't let us out to go to the toilet, using the potty all the time – it just seemed pointless. Why were they so wicked? They'd be walking around, laughing and joking – their keys rattling. And you'd say 'Oh can I go to the toilet?' And their policy is – you let one out you have to let everyone out. So what? I had an adjudication and the governor gave me a terrible punishment, she gave me 14 days' loss of remission, 14 days down the block and 14 days' loss of pay and this was just for kicking my door. I wasn't the only one. That was the punishment she gave all of us. On the adjudication I was very upset. I stood up and I was banging the table. You know you don't realize what you're doing. It must have looked like I was climbing over to grab her. They all just jumped on top of me and I was defending myself and in defending myself I bit an officer and I lost 28 days for that. And the rumour just went round that Alice tried to attack the governor. You don't sort of think 'No I didn't' or 'I did'. You just think 'Oh sod them, let them think what they want to think'. But when I went back and done my three years the big issue was there, the same thing – and I never, never

tried to attack her. Until this day I bet they still believe that I tried to attack her.

The minute I walked in the gate for my three years the same officer I lost the 28 days for biting was the officer in reception, so it was 'Oh gosh!' I felt so ashamed to think that I was coming back for three years to face all these same people and she said to me 'What's your name?' And I said 'You know my name'. 'Don't you start' she said to me and I knew, I just knew it was going to bc hard and so I just decided to be different, to be myself really. I think the officers didn't like it because they thought I was scheming. They thought 'Oh she's using her head now' – and I was just being myself. I was being quiet – because I wanted to get out quickly – and I got my parole. Done 14 months. I got parole. My parole came late, they didn't tell me for three weeks before the date which was 21st December. I didn't have anywhere to go. I had no where to go – so I had this parole date but no home and it was Christmas so you can imagine – the last thing on anyone's mind is where to live. But my probation officer, he was lovely – he found somewhere for me to go.

Actually I went to stay in a friend's flat. She wasn't there but he'd vetted the address for a home leave so that was OK for parole. I was there on my own. That Christmas it was really nice but it was lonely and the high I should have been on I wasn't – Christmas '88. I was just in a daze really, I wasn't sure what I wanted to do. I did think about doing crime again even though I was on parole. As far as I'm concerned they can send me to prison as many times as they like it's only me who can decide if I want to give up crime. They can only incarcerate you for so long and then you're free again. Well you're always free really your body's just there but your thoughts and your feelings are your own. No one can really change that, and my thoughts and my feelings were confused, because the cars and the clothes and the going out and everything were a comfort to me, a material comfort. I belonged, I had something, I achieved something, I could go and make all this money and a lot of money and I was successful at it and also people around me knew and that made me feel good too. It was hard but I knew I had to do something with my life. I met this man and we started seeing each other. Then he found out I'd been in prison and he said he didn't mind because he'd met me before he found out I'd been in prison. He couldn't imagine me being there. It was a bad mistake really because I should have got on with my own life instead of having a relationship. I didn't have time to concentrate on me. I'm very clingy in relationships. I'm confused and the relationship just didn't work out and he was my life. He was my total life. I lived and breathed him. It was easier to do that than to be myself. What I was used to doing I was carrying on doing. It was the best relationship I ever had. I started gradually going back into doing things. I tried to go on a course, to have a career for myself because this man believed in me and I didn't believe in myself. I used to get very insecure, I couldn't concentrate, I was thinking that he's out there with a normal girl, living a normal life, who goes to work 9 to 5, he'd much prefer to be with her than me and I didn't realize that things were just being destructive and terrible.

I was on this course and getting back into the money side of it again and then I went to my doctor in April last year telling him I couldn't cope. I thought I was going to crack. They offered me medication again. I said 'I don't want medication'. And they put me on the waiting list for the hospital to see a clinical psychologist. I looked through the yellow pages and I decided to find a therapist for myself. I found one, but the thing was I had to pay £20 an hour. I was doing this course, I was trying to keep up all the time on this course. I didn't tell anyone I'd been to the courts. It was a sports course and I was training to be an aerobics teacher, sports instructor because inside I was a lot into that and I used to help some of the girls take a class. I've always been sort of athletic I thought 'Well, go for it'. But I couldn't cope – I couldn't be myself around these people because I've always had this ghost about me from my childhood, from my stepmother, that's just made me paranoid and insecure and afraid of people and confused. My relations and communications with people are very bad though most probably people wouldn't be able to tell I'm feeling bad. My skin expresses it – its the only thing that really does. My skin expresses me, the rest I fight to hold. Obviously I had to make money for my therapist. I'm talking to her and half the time I would just sit there and cry for the whole hour. It was nice to talk to someone but it was so much pain. Then one day she confronted me and said to me she was interested to know how I was paying for the sessions. Immediately I clammed up because I didn't want to tell her that I was reof-

fending. I didn't go back because I didn't want to be lectured
about it. It was just one thing that I was clinging on to. I don't
know, it's hard to explain – I was clinging to my reoffending
because it was giving me moral esteem or self-esteem – and in
the end I just threw everything up. I stopped doing the course,
I stopped seeing the therapist and I started to go thieving
again. I made a lot of money. In a short space of a month I had
bought a brand new car and I was back to how I was. Around
August last year was when I got into things. And then one
day, September, I pulled up outside my house the police were
waiting for me – 'Are you Alice? We've come to search your
house.' I had a cheque book and card in the car but nothing in
the house and they took the car down to the station. They
didn't charge me, they wanted me to go back so they could
make more enquiries on the car. I went back about two weeks
later and they charged me.

When I came out of the police station, I remember saying to
myself 'I've lost the car and some money, I'm exposed again
to court and maybe to prison, but I'm walking the streets and
I'm free'. It felt good for a change to be free, even though I'd
been nicked and I was walking along I wasn't on remand. I
was physically as well as mentally free – and I really did appreciate it, I really did appreciate it. After that was just hell.

I was prepared to go out the next day and do something and
my boyfriend was horrified – 'What do you mean? Don't you
realize what's happened?' I wasn't on the same level as him
because it was the life I'm used to living, its no big deal for me.
And he was horrified to think that I could be nicked the day
before and go out the next day and be interested in money.
But my life had to go on, and my life had to go on the only
way I knew how. He made me feel guilty so I didn't do it. I
made a promise to him that I wouldn't do it and I didn't. He
just sort of abandoned me. He was not there for me. He shut
his mind to me, he shut his body to me, he shut everything to
me, which he'd done for a long time anyway but this time it
was worse. I couldn't think straight, I couldn't do anything. I
just used to stay in my bed or stay in. I could hardly wash
myself or eat. I didn't know who I could turn to, I couldn't
turn to him, I couldn't turn to my mother or my father. I
couldn't turn to anyone. My friends – they would just throw
their hands up in the air over me because I'm so depressed
and all I could talk about was my boyfriend. I just seemed to
feel ashamed of how I was being and one day I arranged to

meet him and talk. I said 'I think we should finish'. I didn't want to finish, I wanted him to say to me 'No, I'll stand by you and I'll look after you and we'll go through this together'. And he says to me 'Well OK', and he just left me and I was in the worst state ever. I had this court case, I had no money. I couldn't function, I couldn't do anything and I used to call him up and beg him to come and see me. I had a little bit of money left and I went abroad for the weekend and I came back and he wasn't at the airport to meet me and I was devastated. I was just doing all these crazy things. I was just in a depression where I couldn't do anything. When I think about it now, I don't know how I used to wake up and go to sleep. I phoned my probation officer, I wasn't on probation any more. I said 'I need help, I can't cope anymore', and he was stammering on the phone, he didn't know what to do for me because it was the same thing I used to say to him, that I need help but he never realized what sort of help I needed. I phoned my old children's home and I was crying into the phone saying 'I can't cope with these feelings'. I used to phone my mum and she used to be really wicked to me on the phone. Someone suggested the Samaritans so I called the Samaritans and after calling I used to cry and then sometimes they'd call me to check I was alright. Eventually I went to see them because I try to keep some pills and I don't want to die or anything like that. I just don't know what else to do and I called them and they said to me they thought I should come in. And I said 'Well I can't wash' and they said 'Put your clothes on'. This was about the beginning of October last year. Its OK you sit down and talk to someone, but they just think you're a problem and then you have to go. You still have to go out there and face your life and just talking to someone's not enough.

I decided to phone all these different organizations in the hope that I would feel positive about something. I phoned all these different organizations and they were saying they can't do the area I lived in, or you have to pay. All these things I was coming up against. I would phone one and they would refer me to another or a couple more and I would phone them. I was just phoning and phoning and it used to drain me and I used to give up, I just tried to force myself to come out of it. I can't even remember how I came out of it and meanwhile I was praying for my boyfriend to come back to me – the fact that he just abandoned me hurt me so much and then he was seeing someone else. He just told me he had someone else. I couldn't believe it. I couldn't accept that he'd left me, couldn't accept that he'd gone, that he hadn't stood by me.

I saw this one woman and she said to me it's because of the abuse I'd suffered as a child and I need to talk about it. She offered me six weeks' counselling for free, one day a week. I went to see her and I struggled. I just struggled and I was thinking of going to college I was trying to think of things I could do. Then I had voluntary work. I started to do some voluntary work and I thought about college and it's like I just crawled back up. It was hard and I knew I was crawling. I was doing what I was doing because I was hoping that my boyfriend would see that I'd changed and that I was trying and that he'd come back. I told him I was working, I told him all these lies.

I was still calling my mum. We had an argument and she told me how my father treated her – she said he used to beat her and everything. Because she told me something about herself I told her what happened to me and in fact she never knew. She was stunned and I think she felt guilty. She could understand why I behaved the way I did.

I went to court and got 12 months' probation and a £100 fine. I went to the doctors in April, my date to see a psychologist came up around November. So I started to see her. I had my mum back in my life. I was doing voluntary work and starting some courses. Things just picked up for me. My life has changed – it's just stuck in a rut at the moment, you know, because of prison. Prison – going to prison has ruined my life, just ruined my life. I know what happened to me in my youth ruined my life but prison has just put the lid on it. I mean for my future – if I want to work – if I want to mix with certain people – you mention the word prison to them and they're horrified. And with my mum – I'm only in her life because I put myself there, insisted, and sometimes the way she talks to me is very hurtful, like I'm good for nothing and she's ashamed of me. I suppose I pose a threat to their family, not in respect of violence or anything like that but if anyone ever found out that her daughter, who's been kept under cover anyway, for years, has been to prison and that she's got a brother who's schizophrenic and he's in Broadmoor.

I go to St Georges', I see a lady there – she's really nice. She's trying a thing called cognitive therapy on me which is any negative thought you have about yourself you weigh on a scale of 'really do believe' and 'really don't believe' and then

put it down and look at it. Also I'm on probation, I saw my
probation officer for the first time yesterday and she seemed
like a nice lady. It's hurtful to think that I'm 24 and I've still
got probation officers around me and psychologists, it's still
like being institutionalized, like having social workers or
whatever but it's like in a different light because they can be
like friends. It's nice to know that I've always got someone to
talk to and I have a good friend, I do have a good friend,
actually, Cara, she's my good friend.

I'm not afraid of Cara at all. She doesn't know me inside
out but she knows I'm not really a rough person, I've got a big
heart and I'd do anything for anybody. She doesn't take advantage of that. She lives around the corner from me and I can
go there any time. It's time, it's just time. And I feel good. I
feel confident. I just feel pain over one thing. And I'm coming
to terms with that slowly but surely because I suppose that he
was the best relationship I ever had. I don't really miss the
clothes and the money and stuff like that, I don't because
there's other sides to life.

I'd like to establish myself a career and then think about a
family because it's important for me not just to meet someone
and have kiddies, although I'd love to have kids. I'd like to
find out about myself and experience a bit more. I thought
about doing a degree or a diploma.

There's a lot I don't do because I'd have to do it on my own
– I'm just waiting to meet people – Cara has a child – my other
friend has a child. My other friends – it's a quandary – no one
actually believes that Alice has stopped. People still call me
up and say 'Oh hello, I want to talk to you about something'.
I've told them once my decision, obviously they think that was
just the court case. 'Once the court case is over she'll be back.'
It's amusing and I will listen to what they have to say but I'll
say 'No, it's OK, I'm not interested', and in time I know they'll
just forget me or if they care about me they'll say 'What's
going on?' I don't care – if they go, they go and if they stay
they stay – it's up to them.

I've made up my mind that I'm not going to offend any
more and that's not prison that made me choose that, it was
just realizing that you live a certain life and you're destined to
live a certain way. Nine times out of ten children that have
been abused or not brought up right you find them in prison –
but that's not the place. I know you thieve and everything, you
do all the negative things – because you haven't been brought

up positive, so you don't know any better. I just determined
not to reoffend anymore. I'm determined to do this voluntary
work to find out what's good in me, because that's all I want.
But it's just the pain and everything that I can't control in me
and the ghost that haunts me and my fear.

Alice's childhood is marked by abuse, denial of that abuse by
others and by confusion. Her needs are not recognized and her
attempts to articulate those needs are ignored by the response of
officials who doubt her story (the head mistress) or tell her she
may not pick and choose (officials of the DHSS). As a child, Alice
longs to be part of the conventional family, opting for a role within
such a family wherever possible, with unhappy results. Mistreated,
marginalized and unprotected, she is seen, by herself and others, as
the problem. She is moved from one damaging situation to the
next. Her destiny is in the hands of others.

Small wonder, then, that on officially becoming an adult at 18,
Alice has little sense of personal autonomy, and the patterns
established in her childhood are repeated. She falls in readily with
a man who seems to offer her protection and security, and a role
within society as his partner. She still attempts to prove herself a
good and worthwhile person by refusing to leave a violent and
destructive relationship. Despite his behaviour, she feels she is the
one who has to prove that she is worthwhile. As an adult she does
not run away. She has learned the lesson reiterated throughout her
childhood, to her detriment.

Alice's life is characterized by exclusion. She is excluded from
where she wants to be and by the people who matter to her. She
is excluded from the decisions that affect her life. Abandoned by
her mother, ignored by her father, abused by her stepmother and
mistrusted by her head teacher, Alice attempts to construct solu-
tions for herself but her efforts are thwarted. She tries to include
herself, to place herself where she thinks she ought to be, but her
autonomy is denied. She is told that she may not pick and choose,
but learns that others will pick and choose for her. Thus she finds
herself at different times, in a foster home, with her father, with
her mother, in a children's home, in a prison. As a victim of
incest, she is denied the right to structure her response. Having
told her mother about her father's actions she finds that events
proceed not only without her consent but even without her
knowledge.

In talking about herself, Alice articulates the lack of personal
agency, the impaired sense of self that she experienced. She is not

allowed to cause events, even in her own life, which consequently seems to have a momentum of its own:

. . . my life just lived . . .

Excluded by others, Alice has neither the space in which to develop nor a network of people with whom to develop a sense of self and a self-directed life. She is ignored, abused, denied. Her early life shows many attempts at escape by running away. She wants to find a different place. As she becomes an adult, Alice appears to have learned the lesson that she is not the author of her own story – that she may not pick and choose. She centres her life on another – a man who defines her as outside the norm, both as a criminal and as an improper woman. She accepts his definitions and acts in response to these. Living up to the first and denying the second, she feels that her life is out of her control. She abandons any effort to impose a sense of direction:

I was just living a whirlwind of a life – crime and going to clubs – all over the night – taking drugs. I didn't stop to think 'What am I doing?' I just did it. I ended up back in prison again.

Initially Alice is denied a voice in decisions affecting her life, as she grows older she becomes subject to the increasingly punitive control of others. Her attempts to define herself are met with ever fiercer denial. Prison is the ultimate placement which denies her the freedom to develop and respond as an autonomous being. It is the ultimate exclusion, and the ultimate inclusion. She is excluded from a world of choices and included within an all-encompassing regime.

When Alice kicks the door of her cell and so challenges the inadequacy of the space in which she is held, she is subject to further control. When she violates the space around the governor she is further redefined. Once again she abandons the attempt to define herself.

The rumour just went round that Alice tried to attack the governor. You don't think 'No I didn't' or 'I did'. You just think 'Oh sod them, let them think what they want to think'.

Yet Alice never finally gives up. Throughout her life she has attempted to escape from, move out of, the situations in which she has been placed by others. As a child she runs away, she seeks protection. As a young adult she looks for the means to take control, to direct her own life. She seeks psychiatric help but rejects the use of drugs to pacify her in her current situation. She wants to move on, she wants to move out. And she wants to move in. Alice's reactions to exclusion can be seen as attempts to be included. Initially she conjures pictures of a normal home life for a child. Later she wants to be seen as the loving wife and future mother. She is only too aware of her failure to be acceptable as she constructs a contrasting model of conventional womanhood:

> I was thinking he's out there with a normal girl, living a normal life, who goes to work 9 to 5 . . .

This is the person Alice wants to become through changing her life. But change is not easy to accomplish. The decision causes conflict. Crime brings not only material goods but, through the admiration of others, some self-esteem. It also traps her in one specific milieu and risks the further entrapment of prison. The process of change is painful, slow and, with private therapy, expensive. Support in this process is hard for Alice to find. Again she is abandoned by those she hoped would care for her. Ironically, it is criminal activity which provides her with the financial and emotional resources to pursue the therapy through which she hopes to move away from crime. Alice is aware of the contradictions in which she is caught. At times she feels placed beyond all help, shut out and boxed in:

> What happened to me in my youth ruined my life, but prison has put the lid on it.[1]

But Alice continues to try. She is determined to become independent, make her own choices and take control of her life. She has embarked on a number of strategies to achieve this. Continuing her education will, she hopes, empower her in the labour market. Psychotherapy will enable her to deal with her emotions. Probation will help her to avoid crime. In each of these areas Alice has the opportunity of experiencing personal recognition instead of relating in a situation of dependency in which her autonomy is denied.

> It's hurtful to think that I'm 24 and I've still got probation officers around me and psychologists . . . but it's in a different light because they can be like friends.

For Alice one particularly important area of relationship is a new friendship in which she feels confident and valued:

> I'm not afraid of Cara at all . . . she knows I'm not really a rough person, I've got a big heart . . . She lives around the corner from me and I can go there any time.

Alice is included among the people she wishes to join.[2] However, there are also others who wish to include Alice and who try to draw her back to her former life, to be included among the excluded.

Alice stands midway between those for whom the struggle is too hard, the odds too great, and those who have moved on from being controlled by other people and external circumstances to being self-directing. Alice is one of 34 women that I interviewed who face the challenge of rebuilding their lives after prison (see Appendix 2). For these women the goal was to achieve enough control over their lives to avoid returning to prison in the future.

Like Alice, many of the women suffered exclusion in childhood and early life from the people and places which would encourage the development of an autonomous self. With Alice and many of the other women we see the damage done when the development of the autonomous self is blocked and denied, and the result is dependency and a lack of direction. These women now seek to take charge, to take control of their lives. Through their experiences we can construct a reading of the inhibitors and facilitators of change. We can learn something of the structural preconditions for changes in subjectivity.

In the chapters that follow we will see how prison impacts on the lives of women and how they respond to this both within and, more particularly, beyond the prison. The major analytic device used will be Foucault's distinction between inclusionary and exclusionary modes of control. Foucault (1991) presents a picture of contemporary Western society as a 'disciplinary society' in which members are controlled by being included within disciplinary regimes rather than by being punished by exclusion. His thesis is illustrated by reference to contrasting former societal responses to leprosy and to outbreaks of plague. While lepers were set apart or excluded from society, plague victims were contained and regulated within society.

> The leper was caught up in a practice of rejection, of exile-enclosure; he was left to his doom in a mass among which it was useless to differentiate; those sick of the plague were caught up in a meticulous tactical partitioning . . . The leper and his separation; the plague and its segmentations . . . The exile of the leper and the arrest of the plague do not bring with them the same political dream. The first is that of pure community, the second that of a disciplined society.
>
> (Foucault 1991: 198)

Exclusion or exile removes the contaminating elements from society. Inclusion or containment seeks to render them harmless. In the disciplinary society the members learn self-control through the various institutions in which they are included. In schools and factories, hospitals and asylums, individuals are observed, examined and documented. Those who deviate are subject to correctional procedures in order to induce the internalization of ideologically dominant norms, to 'normalize' their behaviour. Those who continue in their non-conformity risk exclusion. This is the fate of those who display an inappropriate control of self: they become subjected to the overt control of others. They experience the prison. However, in the disciplinary society the prison is seen both to exclude and to include. The prisoner is excluded from the wider society, but is included in an even more intense disciplinary regime, the aim of which is to produce control where other institutions have failed. The prison is the ultimate disciplinary institution. It is total in its embrace. Quoting Baltard, Foucault (1991: 235) says:

> the prison has neither exterior nor gap; it cannot be interrupted, except when its task is totally completed; its action on the individual must be uninterrupted: an unceasing discipline. It carries to their greatest intensity all the procedures to be found in other disciplinary mechanisms.

Ironically, those who are most likely to experience the totality of the disciplinary regime of the prison are those who have already been subject to the official intervention of disciplinary agents in their lives. Such intervention has the explicit aim of normalizing the individual. However, the more the individual is subject to the scrutiny of the disciplinary regimes, the more documentation is compiled, the further the individual is removed from self-control and autonomy within society. The more intense the exercise aimed at inclusion, the greater the likelihood of exclusion – an exclusion from self-directed social interaction but not from the social interaction of the disciplinary agents.

In his discussion of the disciplinary society, Foucault neglects the gendered character of that discipline (Sumner 1990). However, a close examination of the disciplinary institutions reveals that the disciplined subject is also a gendered subject. Normalization involves the acceptance of norms by which sexualities are constructed and ranked hierarchically. In this process a hegemonic masculinity is prioritized, preferred forms of femininity are subordinated, and alternative femininities and masculinities are marginalized (Connell 1987). Thus through formal and informal mechanisms, through discourse and through force, the state plays a part in the construction of womanhood. Within the prison the range of acceptable models of femininity for prisoners is severely limited to those which manifest docility and subservience. The control of women both inside and outside the prison is mediated by concepts of gender. It is as women that they occupy a social space both within and beyond prison. It is as women that they are subject to control and it is as women that they must find self-direction.

For Alice, and for the others subjected to the totality of the prison regime, the problem is one of finding a space in which to construct and develop autonomous selves, to move from containment to empowerment and to become the authors of their own stories. They want to break free of the carceral net and remain free.

In the chapters which follow we will see how these women act, as both constructing and constructed subjects, during and after prison. Chapter 2 shows prison to be experienced as a place of both exclusion and inclusion. Women are taken out of society and away from the people and places that characterize their daily lives. Once in prison, the prisoner is subjected to a rigorous process of control. She is initiated into a regime which will completely structure the material and many of the non-material aspects of her daily existence. Whatever sense of self she brings to the reception process will be subsumed into the identity 'prisoner' which that process is designed to induce. She is closed off from the known world but exposed to total surveillance in a new and strange environment. Individuality is challenged and conformity is endorsed. Within the prison the woman is 'taken down' and taught to 'know her place' in a strictly hierarchical institution. Here she may certainly not pick and choose; obedience, not initiative, is the prescribed pattern of behaviour. Within prison the removal of all the props by which she constructed her former life and the imposition of routine and rule bring the woman to a situation in which her sense of self is strongly challenged. She undergoes a process of adaptation to the regime, and within a regime designed to change her she is changed. The processes by which this change is brought about, as the woman responds to the prison, will be the subject of Chapter 3.

The totality of the prison demands a response from the self. From the experiences of the women, four strategies can be recognized. A woman might use one or more of these strategies. The first of these strategies is *withdrawal*. Many women decided that in order to remain untouched by the prison regime they would withdraw from any unnecessary involvement in prison life. Thus they avoided the further intrusion on the self of punishment and discipline. However, they also abrogated personal agency and so conformed to the rules that demanded passivity and obedience. Many women commented that a sense of self so suppressed was not easily recovered after prison. Furthermore, some were unhappy about situations that they had not challenged, and which they had thus appeared to condone.

The second strategy is *retaliation*. For some women a suitable response to a situation in which their adult status is denied is to behave like children. Thus practical jokes and the thwarting of authority are part of their daily life in prison. For some the challenge to authority becomes more forceful. Such women face periods of time in the punishment block. Both strategies, however, while attempting to assert the self, have the potential to endanger the self. Childish behaviour allows the prison authorities to confirm their opinion on the immaturity of prisoners. Challenging behaviour is likely to provoke further discipline and even the removal of the prisoner from the prison to a special hospital.[3]

The third strategy is *incorporation*. Prison hierarchies reinforce a sense of place and subordination. Such hierarchies rank not only staff but also prisoners and are dependent for their maintenance on the acquiesence and support of prisoners. The victimization and marginalization of particular women may afford the self a sense of belonging, and even superiority, as others are subject to even greater exclusion or inclusion. Such strategies, however, actively endorse the regime and reinforce its effects.

The final strategy is *self-mutilation*. Here the prisoner takes control of her body and inflicts on her self more pain than the regime may inflict. Such agency is obviously self-defeating. It not only damages the self but also is likely to render the woman subject to further medical control and redefinition.

Prison affords little space for the development of a sense of self. Or rather the self that is developed in prison is one which is adapted to the prison. How the prisoner self deals with the outside world is discovered on release. This is the subject of Chapter 4. Women coming out of prison bring with them the sense of self that was cultivated in response to the prison. This may well continue to exclude the woman from the world about her. Socialized into prison routine and discipline, many women found it difficult to take responsibility for the most mundane of tasks. A lack of confidence and a loss of competence resulted in a self inadequate to the new situation. Women also felt excluded by the reactions of others, either to a known ex-prisoner or to a generalized idea of what it means to be an ex-prisoner. Each woman faced the twin dilemmas of secrecy and surveillance. To keep her prison past a secret put a distance between her and any new acquaintance. If the secrecy related to employment there was also the risk of further exclusion on discovery. To admit to her prison past usually invited surveillance. Others decided that the woman must be more stringently supervised and subject to greater interrogation. She was excluded from the usual or customary treatment of women, and included with those considered properly subject to greater control. Such attitudes appear to be fostered by the mass media. Depictions of the woman ex-prisoner confirmed stereotyped images of the inadequate and the untrustworthy. Such stigmatization resulted, for many women, in the intrusion of the prison into the outside world, and their further exclusion from this world.

As women in poverty, women ex-prisoners encounter structural blocks to changes in subjectivity. These structural blocks are to be found in the areas of housing; the labour market and educational provision; social services and health.

For many women, it was the organizations run for and by ex-prisoners which provided that space in which to grow out of the prison self. Here they could recognize and move beyond the prison self. Here the women felt included but not confined. Acceptance here was premised on the woman's wish to take charge of her life and stay out of prison. The ways in which this is accomplished are discussed in Chapter 5.

Despite the exclusion and denial of their early lives, compounded by the experience of prison, the women I interviewed had managed to take sufficient control of their lives to prevent a return to prison. Over half had dramatically changed their lives. They had developed a sense of self capable of choice and control. These women now felt themselves to be included within society, established as contributing, if critical, members. Such change appears to be due to three main processes which occur in relation to each other, sometimes simultaneously, sometimes sequentially.

Re-direction. In order to return from exclusion, the woman needs an awareness of what must be done to accomplish this. For many women it was important to decide to leave an unsatisfactory relationship, to give up drug use, to acquire an education or training, to find a job. However the success of such decisions to redirect their lives depended on both other processes.

Recognition. Many of the women had, in their own eyes and in the eyes of others, achieved little that was worthwhile. In order to develop a sense of an acceptable self it was important that their presence and contribution was valued by others. Their inclusion was then justified by the response of others. Through recognition they began to think differently of themselves. They recognized their ability to take charge and make choices.

Reciprocal relationships. Probably the most pivotal of the factors contributing to change is that concerning relationships. It was important for the women to move out of disempowering dependency relationships and into relationships based on equality. Traditional gender roles had characterized the lives of many of the women, and these patterns of relating within a hierarchy were reinforced by the prison experience. Moving away from hierarchy towards relationships based on equality was important for the woman's sense of an autonomous self. Treated as an equal by those she respected, she began to see herself as capable of working alongside others and constructing her own life.

Chapter 6 examines the policy implications of the preceding chapters. These implications are considered under the headings of sentencing, prison regimes and post-prison provision.

Notes

1 Alice's image of a lid echoes that used elsewhere when a woman speaks of the sense of entrapment within the carceral regime, experienced as both a prisoner and an ex-prisoner (Carlen *et al.* 1985: 87).
2 Cara is an ex-prisoner who has succeeded in changing her life (see Appendix 2).
3 The Secretary of State for Social Services is responsible under section 40 of the National Health Service Re-organisation Act 1973 for providing and maintaining 'establishments for persons subject to detention under the Mental Health Act 1959, who in his opinion require treatment under conditions of special security on account of their dangerous, violent or criminal propensities.' These are known as 'special hospitals' (Home Office and DHSS 1975: 17).

2

TAKING HER DOWN: MAKING A PRISONER

> The state has a constitutive role in forming and re-forming social patterns.
>
> (Connell 1987: 130)

> I don't think anything can be done that's going to be constructive until they get rid of the way they treat women and see women. If you're not like their women – 'Ah then we've got to make you like our women'.
>
> *Linda*

Having pronounced the sentence in court, the judge traditionally dismisses the defendant with the apposite injunction 'Take her down'. Thus begins a process in which the woman is both literally and metaphorically 'taken down'. She is excluded from society, from all that formerly gave her an identity. She becomes a prisoner – depersonalized, degraded, denied any control over her day-to-day existence. She is defined as subordinate: the lowest in a hierarchy and now totally subject to the authority of others.

Such formal control is used on those who have escaped the informal control of ideology – the acceptance of dominant models of normality. These models are justified as 'natural' while operating politically to underpin the current social order for women. One aspect of the dominant ideology is a model of family life and gendered behaviour in which women are defined as domestic in their concerns and subservient to men at home and at work (Eaton 1986). This model of the family, ideologically dominant but not empirically prevalent (Glendinning and Millar 1987: 11), is characterized by a traditional division of labour in which the man provides financially for his economically dependent wife and children and the woman is responsible for the care of family members. The consequences of the dominance of such a model are that women are marginalized in education, the labour market and social space since they are defined as primarily home-centred in their concerns. They are subject to poverty since the male provider, even when present, cannot be forced to contribute to the household finances (Eaton 1986: 60). Furthermore, the jobs available to the majority of women are poorly paid: there is an assumption that they are otherwise financially supported. The dominant model of family life also subjects women to isolation, and coercive control, within the family since there is a reluctance on the part of others (police, neighbours, friends) to interfere in family matters. The consequence of this ideologically dominant model of family life is a greater control of women. Such a model justifies their financial and emotional dependence. Women who accept a gender role defined within this model are subject to the informal control of that model. Their behaviour may be seen as 'natural', arising from biological imperatives, but it reflects and reproduces the gender divisions on which society is based.

In a liberal democracy formal control by the repressive state apparatuses is usually reserved for those for whom informal control by ideology has failed (Althusser 1971). Those women who do not demonstrate control within the ideologically dominant model of the family are most likely to be subjected to state intervention in their lives (Kruttschnitt 1982; Carlen 1988).

Of the 34 women that I interviewed, none, at the time of her arrest, was living within the conventional family model characterized by a gendered division of labour, that is to say, none was living in a heterosexual relationship in which, in return for domestic labour, she received financial support. Each woman had at least one, and usually more, characteristics that further removed her from this model, that excluded her from conventional womanhood. Eight of the women are black. In a racist society they are objects of extra surveillance and heightened suspicion. Three of the black women and 13 of the white women were involved in the use of prohibited drugs and thus moved within drug cultures which supplied not only the substances but also the cultural support for their use and, as such, could be seen as providing an alternative to conventional lifestyles. Seven of the white women and one of the black women had had early experience of state intervention in their lives in the form of official care. Such early intervention renders women vulnerable to further intervention (Carlen 1988: 73–106). Ten of the women were differentiated by their sexuality; as lesbians, they did not conform to a conventional gender role. Four of the women had lived at the peace camp at Greenham Common. They had made a political choice to set themselves apart from conventional domesticity and to undertake active political protest against the presence of nuclear weapons. The 34 women had taken a variety of non-conforming paths, or had been set on such paths – many had little choice in their circumstances. Their exclusion had already begun. Prison may be seen as a place which confirms the exclusion and defines the excluded in entirely negative terms.

Reception

Whatever the circumstances that brought these women to the prison, the process of reception is one which conducts them out of their former status and their old identities as it strips them of their possessions, their clothes and their dignity, and gives them a prison number, a prison identity. They have less than they had, they are less than they were – the 'taking down' has begun. Personal belongings are taken and itemized. The woman is allowed to keep with her only those items specifically listed. She is then given a superficial search before being left to wait for the next stage. She has been taken into the prison and is now held there: the disorientation and confusion which follows is a foretaste of the prison regime. Women described how a complicated routine is followed by staff who assume a knowledge that the first-time prisoner does not have. Women described feeling distanced, unable to accept what was happening, until the new regime was made all too real to them. Judith's experience is typical of many:

> Well it was totally nothing I had ever expected. I didn't know anything about prison, I had never read anything about prison. I was sitting there in total amazement, watching this happen to me. I wasn't actually participating in it. It was total isolation from it. I was in shock, sitting in a room with chairs, in dressing gowns, so called, with your clothes folded up beside you, with women who appeared to know each other and didn't know you.

During reception the prisoner sees a nurse and a doctor but there is usually no medical examination. She also sees members of the prison staff who check details of appearance and property and she is strip-searched. For the women interviewed the strip-search was a significant and distressing experience. The woman prisoner stands naked before uniformed guards with keys – the literal and symbolic tools of her control. She has nothing to protect her. In the closed and secret world of the prison she is laid bare. In future at any time, day or night, she may be subject to the gaze of the guards. With such scrutiny comes control. Her total visibility at this stage prefigures the total surveillance of the future. Furthermore, the brutality of the procedure overrides attempts to distance the self from the situation:

> I put on this act that I was hard, prison was nothing to me, I wasn't scared and I was going to get through. I went to prison in one of the little cubicle vans, like a van but inside its got lots of cubicles. You were locked in. You sit there in a cage until you get to the prison and file out. Although I'd pulled myself together to a certain extent, it was still like a dream, it wasn't like it was really happening, it was like I was taking precautions in case it really was happening. I was chatting away with the other girls like it was a normal thing, an everyday thing to go to prison. And when we were going through reception we had to take all our clothes off and do a twirl in front of the officers. I'd never experienced anything like that before in my life – absolutely stripped naked with nothing, nothing at all, not a ring, nothing. And you had to stick your arms out and twirl. You do it because there's all these people in uniform there and you're frightened that they'll pounce on you if you don't and they probably would if you didn't anyway. I think that woke me up a little bit, after that I was really frightened.
>
> *Cara*

The 'taking down' process continues as the woman is deprived of the agency she previously exercised. Within the prison she loses control of her own life, and the responsibility for others that so frequently accompanies the status of adult woman in society.

> On the outside you get up and you have things to do. You are responsible for a household. You go to work, you pay your rent, you pay your electricity bills, you pay your gas bills. You have the kind of responsibility where you have to keep a home going for your children. You have something to do. In there it's all taken away from you totally. You're like a shell,

you no longer feel human, humane any more, you feel like an empty shell, just a thing that is moving around, it hasn't any heart, no head.

Paula

With no object for her activity, with no purpose in her life, she feels deprived of feelings and thoughts. And this sentiment was echoed by others, such as Beverley, who found in such deprivation the likelihood of future difficulties in coping outside prison:

If you let the system get to you that's when you lose. You can't cope with things outside. You won't cope as you did before because everything's been done. Cooking and things are done for you, everything's done for you – when you must eat, when your door's open.

The prisoner loses the authority to act without the permission of another. To take a bath, to get an aspirin, to borrow a book she needs the authority of someone else. The simplest of actions is curtailed by regulation.

All activities and events are planned, and take place, in time controlled by others. Time acquires a different meaning. It is something over which the women have no control, and yet it is something that they 'do'. Unable to act on their own behalf, unable to plan, to develop, to grow, many women felt excluded from reality. They were cut off from the means to order their lives meaningfully: they felt suspended in time.

You see, prison is really a stopping of time and when I was in there it was a hindrance. It stopped time for me. I was in there for four months when I could have been out here working on myself and working in the real world. Now this is the thing with prison, you know, it's not a real world, it's not a real-life situation, it's far from it and it disorientates you somewhat and it drags you back. It stops, time stops.

Laura

Taken out and taken down, the woman no longer knows who she is or where she is. Prison is not a world in which the self can be an active agent. Furthermore, the prisoner's relationship to the outside world suffers a distortion:

Eventually you forget what the outside is really like. It just becomes a fantasy. It's like light at the end of the tunnel – you just build up this fantasy about the outside world, you only remember the good things.

Cara

Disempowered by the prison regime, the woman begins to romanticize the possibilities of life outside the prison. In prison she can do nothing, to compensate she fantasizes that outside anything is possible. On leaving prison, Fran had a job with British Rail but the reality of her situation was not enough to dispel the dreams engendered in prison.

When you're in there the outside reality becomes a fantasy. You bring that fantasy world out with you and for all I was cleaning trains, I still thought 'Look out world here I come!' – all the things I was going to do and achieve.

When familiar routines and the previous autonomy are disrupted the process by which women become prisoners begins. In this process women are exposed to the twin disciplines of institutional rule and the informal control of other prisoners.

Rules and regulations

The confusion engendered by the reception process continues. Prisons are rule-governed but copies of these rules were difficult to obtain. Official rules which may be available on request are supplemented by standing orders and circular instructions which are not readily available to prisoners.[1] Furthermore, the rules, which are general in their wording, are interpreted in a manner which serves the continual construction of the woman as a prisoner, lacking autonomy or self-direction, subject to the arbitrary decisions of others. Because the rules are not clearly understood, or because the rule that is understood is that women merely do as they are told, there is, for the women, more confusion and greater misunderstanding. Prison rules were experienced not as means of clarifying the social situation but as a way to continue the disempowerment of the woman, the destruction of the former self, the taking-down process.

Women felt that they were not expected to be proactive, and suspected retribution if they were:

Whilst I was in the army I became a barrack-room lawyer and of course when I went into prison I wanted to know my rights as a prisoner and so I asked for the appropriate pamphlets, books, whatever. And of course to get them you have to make a governor's app. and that all goes down in a little book. They don't want you to get hold of the rules and regulations.

Sandy

Certainly most women experienced rule enforcement as capricious and focused particularly on women who did not conform to the expected or appropriate behaviour pattern. The woman in prison is expected to be docile and dependent. Any variation from this extreme version of a gender stereotype is treated with suspicion. Thus women give accounts of the use of discipline to subjugate any expression of self-possession or self-direction.

I thought the way to behave was with dignity (*laughs*), but I got turned down on parole. And the prison governor, who was very good, said to me 'I think you need for their [the officers'] sake, to show a bit of remorse, or they're going to give you a hard time on the way, they want to see you crack'. There is that sort of mentality. You mustn't be seen to survive it, or they feel they're not doing their job in some way.

Bernice

Women are required to play out their subordinate role in relation to legitimated authority. The rules are employed to punish those who do not.

I began to have problems. When you are in prison if you are a particular way they will get to you or try to break you down. And they did try and break me down. They sacked me from my job in prison. They took away all that. I was working in reception as a blue band. And I got sacked from there for a very petty reason.

Paula

Such victimization of those who manifest an unacceptable demeanour is particularly noticeable in cases where women's sexuality transgresses, or poses a threat to, traditional gender roles. Lesbianism constitutes a major challenge since it constructs women without reference to men.

Oh they'll put you on report for anything. Look the wrong way at someone and you're on report. It was open season on me because I got involved with an Arab girl, a PLO girl. They didn't like that, they tried to split our friendship up. To make it more difficult they got us on report, put us behind the door, you know. I mean they could find unauthorized material in any cell – one book too many and they'd put you on report.

Sandy

By creating a taboo (lesbian activity) the prison authorities undermine not only woman-directed sexuality but also other manifestations of solidarity and support among the women. To reinforce the dependence (on legitimated authority) and the docility of the women, the regime proscribes manifestations of mutuality.

At Styal, there was this rule, it wasn't a written rule, this lesbian activity rule, which, when I was there was really being brought up quite a lot. Houses were being split up and women moved to different houses if there'd been a number of unspecified marks on the body. L.A. could literally mean anything: sitting on a bed, playing cards, giving another woman a hug.

Nicki

The manner in which such rules are enforced is further evidence of a discipline designed to produce conformity and passivity. Cara describes the humiliation and frustration of an adjudication which follows a trivial, but typical, example of reportable behaviour.

One night I was reading the Bible and if I'm reading the Bible I don't talk to anybody. I only read a chapter. While I'm reading that chapter that time is mine, devoted to God. So nobody can disturb me. I was reading a chapter and an officer came in and turned the light off, so I got up and switched it back on and she came up and switched it off. I switched it back on, it was really silly, you know. And she said 'I've switched the light off, do not switch it on again'. And I said 'Look, I'm just finishing, I've got two verses to read, why don't you just let me finish it?' So she said 'No, I'm telling you now, get into bed, I'm turning the light off'. I'd just had enough. She switched the light off and went out. I opened the door so that the light from the corridor would shine on the book and I could finish the last two verses. So she gave me a direct order to get into bed and I just ignored her and carried on reading. Then she went off and the next morning I was adjudicated. The assistant governor, she was mad, she screamed at me worse than my mother ever has in my life, and you can't answer back. I had to sit in this chair, pushed under the table with my arms on my lap, two officers on either side. The assistant governor was screaming so much that the spit from her mouth was catching on my face. She was bright red. I thought 'That's it, she's going to take the whole of my remission'. And at the end of it all it was a caution. When I came out of that office I was in tears, I was shaking, really angry. Everything had been taken away from me. Dignity, everything, it had all gone and I couldn't say anything on my own behalf, scream back or tell her to shut her face or anything.

Cara

In this incident we see how the endorsement of the power structure within the institution takes priority over the explicit aims of the institution. Prisons were originally planned to bring about a change of heart in wrongdoers (Ignatieff 1989). For the early penal reformers, this involved attempts at religious conversion. How ironic, then, that a woman's attempt to create some space for religious observation should become the cause of her condemnation. Of course, in the eyes of the officer and other members of the institution, Cara's offence lay in attempting to create a space for herself – in attempting to impose her own definition on a situation. In prison she has to learn that time and space and action are to be defined by others. This lesson is driven home as she sits pinioned and silenced in the face of the fury of the governor. The final sentence is light – the real punishment is the denial of her dignity and the demonstration of her powerlessness before the authorized agents of social control.

Women prisoners are more likely than men to be subject to further discipline within the prison. In 1989 the average number of punished offences was 2.7 for women and 1.6 for men (Women's National Commission 1991: 25). This is a pattern which has persisted over the years and reflects the greater control to which women are subject, and the narrower range of options available to them.

Medication: drugged to docility

I was naive to what prisons would be like. I had this idea that there would be people in there that'd be helping.

Bernice

When I was in Holloway I was under a psychiatrist for depression, but they just give you medication, they don't really do anything constructive with you.

Norma

Among those interviewed there were women who had looked to prison to help them change. Feeling their lives to be out of control and on a destructively downward spiral, they had hoped that official intervention would help them to find other ways of understanding and acting. Accepting the dominant explanations of women's non-conforming behaviour, they were prepared to accept a diagnosis of individual pathology. However, they were not prepared to accept that medication was the appropriate treatment. Like Alice in Chapter 1, they saw drugs as destructive, useful only for altering mood or masking symptoms. Real change required a different response.

> It would have been very easy to be like some of the girls and escape with drugs.
>
> *Alice*

The phenomenon of 'doing your bird on your pillow' or 'sleeping your time away' is familiar to prisoners. But excluding herself from the situation does not allow a woman to achieve control over the situation; rather it furthers the prison's control of the woman. As in the outside world women are more likely than men to be clients of the National Health Service, so women prisoners are more likely than men to be clients of the Prison Medical Service (NACRO 1986). The figures published in the Prison Department *Annual Report* indicate that more drugs are dispensed to women than to men. Genders and Player (1987) note that between January 1984 and March 1985 women received five times as many antidepressants, sedatives and tranquillizers. They suggest that the prescription of medication for women was one way of acclimatizing women to the prison regime:

> many prescriptions were issued for women who were not diagnosed as being 'sick' . . . the women were described as having 'normal' difficulties in coping with problems associated with their imprisonment, and medication was seen as helping to alleviate some of the more acute pain they were suffering.
>
> (Genders and Player 1987: 165)

The medical regime may be seen as a part of the system of control by which a woman is defined by others and denied her own authority. In a rigorous analysis of the role of the Prison Medical Service over the last 200 years, Joe Sim (1990: 129) concludes:

> Criminal women have been a central concern for prison managers and medical and psychiatric professionals since the

emergence of the modern prison system at the end of the eighteenth century . . . While medical and psychiatric professionals were central to the lives of women prisoners, they should be seen as part of a wider professional network whose concern with returning criminal women to their 'normal role' legitimised a level of intervention and surveillance which was much more intense than that experienced by criminal men.

The gendered nature of the expectations concerning appropriate behaviour is particularly noticeable in special hospitals where women are expected to manifest appropriate behaviour as an indicator of sanity:

> They used to have discos and they used to scrutinize you, watch every move you made and it was so horrible. It was like you were animals in cages. That's why I never used to go out. I said 'I refuse to go out there and they do that to me'. Then [a nurse] said to me 'Look you had problems with men in your life, so they are going to watch you specially. Go out there and try and have a nice time, because if you're not seen to be mixing, you're not ready [to be discharged].'
>
> *Bella*

When the new Holloway Prison was opened in 1977 the architecture reflected official policy at the planning stage. Women criminals were to be subject not to punishment but to individualized psychiatric treatment. It was assumed that the numbers of imprisoned women would fall as the end of the century drew nearer. However, there was a rise in numbers and this coincided with a change in policy. More explicit forms of control became dominant again. The medical model which persists is one which fits happily with the institutional aims of containment and control. Drugs are administered for this purpose (Sim 1990: 164–76). This was recognized by Bernice, Norma and Alice. But the more explicitly therapeutic regime to which Bella was exposed was also concerned with control. Like an animal in a zoo, Bella is required to exhibit the appropriate characteristics of tameness or domestication before she will be allowed out.

Education

The education department was one aspect of the prison regime which no woman felt to be coercive or degrading. In some cases

prison provided the woman with the opportunity to obtain skills
and qualifications:

> I did a typing course and got a couple of certificates. I did
> Community Care and they sent me out on a course.
>
> *Hazel*

For others the prison education department provided an introduction to their own potential to be developed elsewhere:

> I went to Drake Hall and got right into education and it was
> great. It was really helping me. The Education Officer, he said
> 'It's about time you started to say to yourself that you are
> intelligent, you can do things'. That was really good for me.
>
> *Laura*

> I loved the Education Department. I came out thinking 'Well,
> I want to pursue my education'. I wanted to learn more.
>
> *Kathy*

However, women frequently complained that too often their
access to education was disrupted by the prison regime.

> It was 23½ hours bang up in there [Risley]. When you went
> down to get your dinner and take it back to your cell, you'd
> see a sign saying 'Do you want education? Learn to read and
> write. Go and see the Education Officer'. You couldn't get out
> of your bloody cell door to go and see them.
>
> *Laura*

Many saw education as a means of self-development and self-
empowerment, and, for this reason likely to be easily withdrawn by
the prison authorities or subject to disincentives:

> [there were] things which I would've loved to have done in
> prison and could never afford to – typing and computer
> courses, they're always the lowest paid because they feel
> you're getting something. I always went for the highest-paid
> jobs because I never ever wanted to ask my family to send me
> money.
>
> *Meg*

Education may be seen as one area of prison life through which it
is possible to ameliorate the general trend of prison experience.
Through education, women may acquire skills which will empower
them and facilitate their re-entry into society. Of the 34 women

interviewed, 11 considered education to be an important tool in gaining control over, and changing, their lives. However, only five of the women recognized the prison education department as significant in their lives. The education departments that these women had encountered were stimulating and the teachers were motivating. But for the majority of the women, movement from one prison to another, curtailment of classes, and a need to earn more money denied them the opportunity of exploring their own capabilities. The potential of the prison education department is thwarted by the context in which it operates.

Discipline and gender

Beginning with the reception process, prison routine and prison practices may be understood as defining a particular role for women prisoners. The gendered nature of this role becomes even more apparent when the women are considered in relation to men and to children within the prison. Here women excluded from society are forcefully included within narrow definitions of gender. Furthermore, prison inverts the gendered relationships. For many of the women I interviewed family life was characterized by the absence of men and the presence of children. Prison is characterized by the presence of men and the absence of children.

1 The presence of men

As Sim (1990) has demonstrated, the division of labour within women's prisons has traditionally reproduced the sexual divisions of the wider society. Male governors and male doctors (sometimes the same person) have prescribed and supervised the treatment to which women prisoners are subject. However, a recent innovation in English prisons has heralded an increase in the direct control of women by men. Male officers now work inside women's prisons. This practice began in 1986 when 16 male officers took up their posts in Holloway Prison (Tchaikovsky 1986). Previously male officers were posted at the gates and were only to be found working inside the prison when summoned to assist with a 'difficult' prisoner (see O'Dwyer and Carlen 1985: 148).

For women, the routine employment of male officers involves a continual and immediate definition of their gender role in relation to men.

He was a big sweaty man, and there were a few prisoners he'd
really horse-play with; and he made funny comments all the
time. He'd lean up against the doorway so you had to squeeze
past him and he had a big gut and he was just like ugh! And he
just made comments all the time.

Martha

These 'comments' were continual reminders of the hierarchy involved in the traditional gender roles. In the following example the
man justifies his involvement in a specifically female concern by
presenting himself as a father, a male in a traditional gender role
involving authority over women. The remark also serves to indicate that there is no matter over which he has no jurisdiction:

He was Head of Wing, and there's a trolley in the hall where
you have to go if you want to pick up sanitary towels or
something and if you want them you had to go to the office.
Instead of some woman there was this total thug. I mean I'm
not squeamish but you don't necessarily want to talk about it
with him. He'd say 'It's alright, I'm a father too'.

Martha

Here the male officer stands in authority over the most powerless
of women – the female prisoner – and demonstrates her total
vulnerability. This becomes even more apparent in the case of the
women held in special hospitals. The presence of a man redefines
the situation. The violence becomes gendered and takes on the
characteristics of rape:

There was a man on our ward, a male staff, he practically
raped the women on the ward. If they were putting on strip
dresses, because they were fighting, he would practically rip
their clothes off until they were naked in the passage, and
whip on one of those horrible strip dresses. I mean he raped
her. Do you understand what I mean? And then he flung her
in a room and shut all the shutters so it was total darkness,
then he used to laugh about it and find it very funny. I used to
hear him laugh when he stripped off a woman and flung her
in, I used to hear him laugh. But he certainly raped her, he
did, although he didn't do anything physically.

Bella

If the situation in Holloway, described by Posen (1988), is rep-
licated elsewhere, then many women prisoners have already experienced violence from men, including rape, before they reach

prison. The presence of men reiterates a model of coercive control with which they are already familiar. Thus the addition of gender as a factor in dominance reinforces a lesson that has implications beyond the concern for good order within the institution. It reveals and reinforces patterns of authority, based on gender divisions, which are found throughout society.

However, it is not their maleness alone which makes the men so effective in inculcating an acceptable or docile femininity in the women prisoners. It is maleness within a hierarchy, functioning so that both are endorsed – the prevalence of hierarchy and the relative subservience of women. Where men did not exploit the potential offered by the regime they endorsed neither patriarchy nor hierarchy. Martha, who had been critical of the presence of male officers, was appreciative of the attitude of a man from the education department.

The nicest person, the nicest non-prisoner, was a man, in the education department. If you are in a single [cell] it's normal – you know the little hatches on the door, either you just see two eyeballs, or the hatch slams down and you get a face pushed through and someone's screaming something at you or chucking something through the hatch. And the first thing I knew there was a knock on the hatch, I thought, 'What's going on?' And I went over and opened the hatch and he was standing right across the corridor, doing the sort of equivalent of 'Are you at home?' It was actually nice to be dealt with by someone who wasn't being pushy.

Here the man does not intrude his presence upon the woman. He keeps a distance and allows her the control over that distance. However, such encounters were rare in the prison experience of the women. In the majority of cases, interaction with members of staff, male or female, reinforced the prison hierarchy and the powerlessness of the women prisoners. The inclusion of the women is forced. Where the member of staff is male the women's subordination and forced inclusion is gendered. Their powerlessness in relation to men is emphasized.

2 The presence and absence of children

Prison Rule 9 states:

The Secretary of State may, subject to any conditions he thinks fit, permit a woman prisoner to have her baby with her in prison and everything necessary for the baby's maintenance and care may be provided there.

Of the 12 prisons for women in England and Wales, three have facilities for mothers to keep their babies with them (NACRO 1988). In Holloway babies may stay until they are nine months old. In Styal, also a closed prison, babies usually stay until they are nine months old but recently there have been cases of women in special circumstances keeping their babies up to the age of 18 months. In Askham Grange, an open prison, babies may stay for up to two years.

Given the significance of motherhood in dominant models of femininity, it is important to examine the role of the prison in relation to mothers. Perhaps the severest enforcement of gender roles is to be seen in the position of mothers with babies in prison. From the pregnancy through the birth to the child care within the prison, women are routinely reminded of their status as prisoners and therefore inadequate mothers. While their interaction with men involves enforced inclusion, their interaction with children involves exclusion from their gender role – or rather, exclusion from their definition of the gender role. The prison authorities define the role that the women will play in relation to their children.

I was put into an ordinary wing which I thought was a bit weird, because the first three months are supposed to be the worst. At five months I went into the hospital wing and then on to the mother and baby unit.

Carole

Each time I'm pregnant I'm very ill and I went down the mother and baby wing until I was sentenced. Some of the officers there were nice and some were horrible. It's just ridiculous, they want you to go down on your knees and scrub floors. It's terrible. I was put on report. This officer said 'Take these bags' and I said 'No, I'm not taking it', she says 'Well, I'm going to put you on report'. If I wasn't pregnant I would have gone down the block. I got loss of pay.

Rene

Babies are not born within the prison, nevertheless the prison, symbolized by two accompanying officers, follows the mother out to a local hospital so that her baby is born in conditions approximating incarceration. Worse still for the women, their prisoner status is on display outside the prison:

I've gone into labour and gone into hospital and I've got two prison wardens with me 24 hours, even in the labour ward. I had one either side of me. And I've never felt so horrible in my life, because it was an ordinary ward, I wasn't even on a side ward. And I had these two screws next to me and they were supposed to come in civvy uniform – but you could tell. I had the baby at one o'clock in the morning and the next day they shipped me back to Holloway, and it was horrid, just horrid. I remember looking at her and all the bare walls and thinking 'You poor little mite, we're in prison now'.

Carole

Here we have the ultimate merging of inclusionary and exclusionary devices. Women are, at the same time, both within and out of prison, both out of society and in society. They are mothers with no control over their child's nurturance, yet they are responsible for their child's situation in prison.

Yes, the officers go with you. And I tell you it's horrible, because all these people having their babies. They must have said to themselves, 'Well why are those two ladies here day and night with this person?'. It's horrible. The worst time for me was when I had my baby, and I had to take her back into Holloway. I looked at the cell. How could I bring my child back here?

Rene

Once back in prison, both mother and baby are subject to the full rigours of prison discipline:

In my eyes she wasn't my baby at all. She was HM Prison Holloway's, because I couldn't do what I wanted. I was told what to give her. And when she started on solids, she was on one rusk and she wanted more than that. I knew she did. It took two weeks to get her another rusk. Six bottles a day, you had to make them up in the morning, stick them in the fridge, and put your initial on top. And if you wanted any more that was it, because the stuff was all locked up.

Carole

The full impact of prison becomes apparent when the child encounters the outside world for the first time. One mother tells how she was allowed two hours' parole to go out from the prison to cash a child benefit giro. In her apprehension at encountering the outside world, the mother overlooked the fact that her child knew nothing beyond the prison in which she had lived since birth:

I was scared, I'd never been out for 16 months, and I thought 'Well, what am I going to do?' I never thought about little Emma. Of course she's in her buggy and all the cars are going by and she's like this [rigid with fear], holding on to her buggy. And I thought 'Yeah, I forgot about the cars and all that'. She couldn't understand it. It was all too much for her and it was for me as well. We were glad to get back. I ran down Holloway Road. I never even thought about that for children but, good God, it must've been like going into a different world.

Carole

By taking and including the prisoner's child in the world of the prison, the pain of exclusion now relates to the leaving of prison. For Carole's daughter there was a further trauma in store. Having spent her first 11 months in the closest proximity to her mother, she then had to suffer total separation from her. Carole was refused parole and became so angry at the decision that her behaviour resulted in a transfer from Askham Grange, an open prison, to Styal which is closed. The child went into care for six weeks.

Donzelot (1979) has discussed the way in which state involvement in family life works for the reproduction of society. This involves, primarily, a relationship with the mother. Agents of the state (doctors, welfare workers, teachers) work with those women who manifest the most acceptable maternal role – usually middle-class women. Working-class women, especially those who give rise to suspicion that their child-rearing practices are unacceptable, are likely to become the objects of surveillance by the same agents of the state. For women in prison, who are even further removed from acceptable models of femininity, the state becomes even more directly involved in their maternal role. Control is taken from them. However, they are inducted not into an acceptable mother role, but into incompetence. They are not permitted to act as mothers.

Many mothers in prison have to leave their children outside. They are removed from being active agents not only in their own lives but also in the lives of those nearest to them. In many cases they endure the frustration of learning that events are overtaking the child and they have no part to play:

Two days before I got bailed, I got a message from a policeman. He came to my cell and said to me 'By the way, your mother just rang up, your daughter's been made a ward of court and her father's got custody', just like that. I was mad. I was trapped in those four walls, no phone, nothing. I just freaked out. It didn't seem possible. I was absolutely amazed that nobody had even contacted me.

Cara

Not only do the mothers have to deal with their own grief about separation but they also have to suffer the pain of their children:

It affected my children physically, mentally, every way. When you have three people, three lives depending on you without a father – disappearing from them, can you imagine it?

Paula

Paula's children were with her mother; nevertheless they suffered, both mentally and physically, from the loss of their mother:

My daughter, she stopped growing for a time, her hair fell out. And I used to get a telephone call to home instead of visiting and when I spoke to them it's as if I am speaking to somebody else. Even the letters that they wrote – my son used to say things to me like 'I've gone to my other planet'. And I used to think he was going mad. And the eldest boy, he wouldn't write. He just refused to write to me.

The suffering of their children was a persistent theme in mothers' discussion of imprisonment:

I had to think about my children. I mean they suffered while I was in prison, mentally, although they were taken care of. I didn't realize my kids loved me so much. You know my little girl's hair was falling out because she had a nervous reaction, because of [my] being in prison. I used to cry and cry and cry because I hated them coming to see me because it used to cut me up inside.

Rene

When women speak of the prison experience they chronicle exclusion: exclusion from home, from family, from friends, from meaningful time, and from all that contributes to a sense of self and self-worth. Furthermore, within the prison they are excluded from decisions relating to their own lives, from autonomy over their own lives, and from the close involvement in the lives of others which contributes to a sense of community. This is the result of a regime which defines these women as different from, and less than, other women – excluded and taken down. How, then, do the women respond to these lessons? In what are they included by that response? What effect does the prison experience have on them? What changes are brought about as the women become prisoners? These are the questions addressed in Chapter 3.

Notes

1 In September 1991 the Prison Reform Trust and the Home Office produced a Prisoners' Information Pack which gives a wide range of useful and up-to-date information for prisoners. This is now distributed at reception to each new prisoner.

3

KNOWING HER PLACE: WOMEN'S RESPONSES TO PRISON

Nothing seemed to touch my emotions, for the whole of the time I was in there I put up this protective barrier. Watching everything, just noting everything. I felt like a piece of fluff on a river, I was going there no matter what happened, and nothing I wanted seemed to come into it. So I just switched off 'need'.

Judith

You come into the system, you can't help yourself. So I just keep on fighting back. I had to fight for myself all the time, it's the only way I know.

Beverley

The prison cannot be ignored. Pushed out, taken in, held down, the women's responses to their situation varied from a withdrawal of the self to a violent reaction to the forces acting on the self. In responding, many women felt that they changed. This chapter examines these responses and changes.

As prisoners, women have always been considered to be notoriously difficult. They are twice as likely as men to be the subjects of official discipline procedures by the prison authorities and their consumption of psychotropic drugs is high (see pp. 29–31 above). Perceiving women as difficult prisoners has led to a number of explanations of their behaviour. Women are intrinsically unsuited to prison, or any non-domestic setting. Women are placed in a prison setting which is unable to respond to their needs because it

is designed primarily for men. Women are disciplined more severely than men because of the double standard concerning acceptable behaviour both within and beyond the prison. Women
who go to prison are incorrigible, have transgressed both gender
norms and legal rules, and so are more likely to require greater
control. Whatever the reasons, the pattern persists. Women are
subject to greater control. Over two-thirds (24) of the women I
interviewed had been put on report at some time. In this they
recognized the prison's response to their response – the escalation
of a process by which they were subject to interactions that defined
them first as prisoners, then as difficult prisoners requiring greater
control.

How did these women understand these experiences and how
did they respond to imprisonment? In discussing their own responses, and those they had observed in others, the women described ways of coping with the regimes in which they were held.
From these descriptions it is possible to identify four different
strategies. Some employed different strategies at different times.
Some of these methods, rather than being described as chosen
strategies, were depicted more as defensive reactions. In all these
moves we can recognize both attempts by the women to find a
space for themselves to retain a sense of self by self-directed activity, and the power of the institution in denying that self by
redefining and so disempowering the women.

1 *Withdrawal*

In Chapter 1 we learned how, during her third sentence, Alice
decided to conform to the prison regime. In this way she hoped to
avoid being subject to the disciplinary measures that she had experienced during her second sentence. To evade the more extreme
forms of institutional control it is necessary to present the self as
already sufficiently disciplined. To preserve something of the sense
of self with which one entered prison it is necessary to withhold
that self from engagement with the world of the prison. This, for
many women, was the way to make a choice, to choose not to
choose. In this way women excluded themselves from involvement
in their own lives and in the lives of others. In attempting to escape
the influence of the prison, they accept the rule which denies self-
direction and responsibility. For many women this became apparent when they reflected on their relationships to others and their
responses to injustice.

Barbara was a member of the Greenham Common peace camp. She is still amazed that she failed to challenge an officer who refused medical aid to a dying prisoner.

> I was standing outside the doctor's room and this woman came along the stairs and I could hear her before she came down the stairs. It was very heavy breathing, a tremendous noise, it was more than asthma. She made her way to the doctor's room and the nurse sent her back up the stairs and she came down again and she sent her back up the stairs. When you're in prison a lot of stuff you take in but you don't always react to it because you're just thinking 'Well what's going on here?'

The woman was found dead in her cell less than two hours later. The case is described in Women's Equality Group/London Strategic Policy Unit (1987: 152–5).

Barbara felt herself disempowered by the confusing totality of the regime, and disengaged from people and events. Olive, however, made a deliberate decision to withdraw in order to preserve something of her self from the influence of the prison. She did not wish to risk further control by breaching prison discipline. Ironically, it was an attempt to prevent disorder that caused her to be accused of rule-breaking.

> I never gave them the chance to do anything to me. I never let them take me down the block. I never let them humiliate me, put myself in a position where they could humiliate me. The only time they took me down was when we were in the showers and the girls were going to do something really stupid and I said 'You can't do that, do it properly. Write a petition, have the girls sign it and do it that way. Have an audience with the governor.' And somebody heard me say something and I was put out for inciting a riot.

In intervening, actively engaging with others to influence future action, she broke the unwritten but enforced rule which denies the self both autonomy and intervention in the lives of others.

Withdrawal from the prison regime means withdrawal from others – the creation of a distance not easily recovered:

> The only thing you can hold back is your anger. You hold back what is you and when you come out you are still distanced. It took me over a year to lose that distance. It took me over a year to lose my temper.

Judith

In withdrawing from the situation, women may feel that they are keeping the institution at a distance, however, they are actively conforming to the regime which defines docility as an appropriate characteristic for women. In withdrawing from the situation, the woman is unable to find a space in which to redefine herself. Instead she is forced to accept the definitions of others.

2 Retaliation

Since prison denies autonomy and authority to prisoners it is experienced by them as a situation in which they are treated as less than adult or as children. Much of the regime reminded women of being the rigid control of a school:

> There are some older women in there and they're treated like children, by women who are prison guards who are young enough to be their children. And it's just so strange, it's like being in a totally enclosed boarding school, with really really petty rules, and very heavy penalties if you break them – and you've got no say.
>
> *Judith*

Many women recognized in their responses behaviour that would confirm the institutional judgement that they were not competent adults.

> Because you get treated like [a child] you start acting like one. You try to get one over on the screws. If you did something stupid, really stupid, you did it just to keep yourself together.
>
> *Cara*

Strategies which would be characterized as immature modes of resistance gave the women the feeling that they were still capable of achieving something. But now their focus was the prison which structured both resistance and conformity.

> I used to get into every kind of skulduggery that was going – like making drink, making alcohol. We put it under the stairs in a staircase that has a lot of air going through. Then you'd pass officers on the stairs knowing that this bucket of hooch was underneath. I used to thrive on that. That was the way I did my prison sentence – messing around and getting them back all the time.
>
> *Lisa*

Such a response gave the women a sense of self-worth and self-control, but such a self was not capable of engaging with the representatives of the institution to bring about change. Accepting the space defined by others, the women acted within that space to confirm the definition (of non-competent adult) imposed by others. But even such apparently unimportant behaviour brought the risk of greater control, of a further restriction on the self. This Cara recognizes:

Everything you are used to doing as an independent human being is wrong and you have to stop yourself from doing it. You can get into serious trouble for very petty things. I got into trouble at Bulwood Hall for throwing a jug of water over somebody else. We were mucking about, playing. It was association. I'd had a bath and somebody, one of my friends, threw a bucket of water over me and she was hiding away from me. Next thing I was grabbed by what seemed hundreds of officers, thrown into a cell, the door was locked and the next morning I was taken down the block and I was scared. I'd heard about this block. All your privileges are removed while you're down there and you are treated like some kind of mass murderer, like the most serious prisoner.

For some women, confrontation with the prison authorities was one way of preserving a sense of self-dignity. However, a high price may be paid for such demonstrations of autonomy. Pushed to extreme behaviour, or placed in a situation where behaviour that seems appropriate to the woman prisoner appears bizarre to the authorities, the woman runs the risk of further definition. She may be diagnosed as mentally ill and thus be subject to the greater control of medication, or the special hospital. In the following account Beverley describes as a victory against the system, an action that might have been diagnosed as evidence of mental disorder.

If you're down the block some times they don't give you baths for days and I hadn't had a bath for two weeks. I like a bath more often when I have my monthlies. They told me to just wash and I got fed up with it. Treat me like a devil. Can't have a bath. If I can't have a bath after having my monthlies, I might as well throw the things out at you. So I started to throw out Tampax, my used things, just sling them at them. Then, eventually, they gave me a bath, because I wouldn't eat or nothing.

The Pyrrhic nature of such victories is recognized by Jo, a woman who spent much of her time in the special hospitals:

> If you're scared shitless you're never going to admit it and the last person you're going to admit it to is you. I've been hit many times by screws and still laughed – with my teeth hanging out still grinned at them. You might have got all the bumps and the lumps but psychologically you're the winner. When they come in next time they're going to come in double strength. You tend to just grin but inside you're literally weeping to death but you just daren't let them know, 'cause otherwise they would win, they would have got you.

Women who retaliate, who appear to resist the prison, run the risk of being beaten by a regime which may change them both physically and mentally. They risk being defined as mad and transferred from prison, where they serve a fixed sentence, to a special hospital and an indeterminate stay.

> Gemma spent six and a half years in Broadmoor. She describes it as 'your worst nightmare. Something they hold over you in prison. You know if you go to a special you can't go any lower. That's it. It frightens you to death because you don't know when or even if you'll ever get out'.

(Stevenson 1989: 14)

Between April 1989 and March 1990 transfer directions were issued for 204 men or 0.4 per cent of the total prison population of men and 16 women or 0.9 per cent of the total prison population of women (Home Office 1990c: 87).

3 Incorporation

Both withdrawal and retaliation allow for the incorporation of the woman into the life of the prison or another even more closed institution. By refusing to act, on her own behalf or on behalf of others, the woman colludes with the denial of her self by abrogating all responsibility. By reacting to the situation she presents herself for further definition and further control. Other forms of response to prison life allow for even greater incorporation of the self by the prison. Women may play an active part in maintaining the hierarchy that characterizes prison life, and so endorse the relative positions within that hierarchy. Experiencing exclusion themselves they practise exclusion on others. Being subject to power, they wield a limited power.

> What I hated more than anything was that there was so much bad feeling and aggression between the women. Styal is split into little houses and at night there's no staff on the houses and so any bad feeling that goes on just gets sorted out at night when there are no officers around. I was in a dorm with a woman who wasn't particularly well liked, the kind you give a number of cold baths to in the middle of the night.
>
> *Nicki*

Prison life does not encourage the creation of community in which a sense of self could develop, in which all would be accepted. Women experience isolation from the outside world, and from each other. Victimization endorses this.

> Pamela was a woman who went around asking people to be her friend. And she would only have a friend on Wednesday at two o'clock when she picked up her canteen and then only for as long as it took to take her Old Holborn and a Mars bar off her.
>
> *Fran*

In such a situation many women felt that they changed in response to perceived aggression from others. If there was to be a hierarchy to be reinforced then they determined not to be at the bottom, not to be victims.

It was difficult to remain unchanged when all around people were defining and redefining the context in which they had to live.

> It's not very nice at all. Even the prisoners, some of them are not very nice as well. Some of them could be really aggressive. You've got to show them that, no, you can't walk over me, you can't take liberties with me.
>
> *Rene*

> I abhor physical violence, but in prison I was totally different. I still abhorred it, but I was much more physical and felt much more physical. It was more like being in care where if you didn't physically stand up to someone who you thought could possibly bully you then you were going to be in trouble. Although I didn't agree with that I was willing to.
>
> *Nicki*

For one woman, Fran, a process of maturation and change had begun before her final prison sentence. Because of this she saw such behaviour differently, and responded differently.

> Going into prison with that more serious frame of mind. I noticed for the first time how very low it was. One example of the lowness was the Holloway treatment, women's heads put down the lav and flush the toilet. I mean you knew those things went on and you couldn't condone them and in fact this particular sentence, which I probably wouldn't have done before, I actively attempted, quite successfully, to stop them. Before I had always identified with the prisoners, this time it was hard to.

The aggression and violence, a product of the prison situation, is often encouraged by the prison officers. They focus such malevolence on individuals whose scapegoat status supports a hierarchy in which there is someone lower than the 'ordinary' prisoner. Women who easily fall into such a category are women who are even more excluded than the ordinary prisoner from acceptable models of femininity and social acceptability. Those accused of harming children are the regular targets of such orchestrated attacks (cf. O'Dwyer and Carlen 1985: 157–8).

> I was sentenced at half past three and by the time I got to Holloway at ten past four, the whole of the wing knew what I was in for. I was thrown down the stairs on one occasion and I had boiling water chucked over me and I decided I would be better off on Rule 43. But it took me nearly four months to be allocated onto the Rule 43 wing. During that time I was on the medical wing as supposedly a normal prisoner but locked in all day because obviously I couldn't go out and mix with the other women.
>
> *Terri*

Another woman was 65 years old when she first experienced not only prison but also the victimization reserved for those who are considered to have committed particularly unacceptable crimes. Doris was accused, with her daughter, of burying another pensioner and claiming her pension. While she was on remand the officers made a newspaper account of the trial available to her cell mates:

> They done a nasty trick, when the papers came out on Saturday it was splashed all over. They put the *Mirror* in and shut

the door so that all the girls could read it. And they were
going to put my head down the toilet. They were going to kill
me. And they're all standing there: 'What shall we do?' I was
frightened, I was scared stiff. Yes, I thought they were going
to kill me. All those big women.

However, not all attempts by officers to set prisoner against prisoner are successful. Women who went to prison as a result of
political action at the Greenham Common peace camps were well
received despite attempts by officers to set other prisoners against
them:

We went onto one wing, there was a funny atmosphere and
one of the women on the wing told us the screws had basically
primed the women – 'Smelly Greenham women coming up
here', what trouble we are.

Martha

Nor was there resentment against women who received more publicity and support than other prisoners:

The first few times I was in prison, it came to me that there
was every reason why a lot of women that I was in with could
feel really resentful, because you're in for a short time and
you have this vast back-up and you know there's somewhere
to go to when you get out, and you know somebody in the
next bed is waiting for a letter from her boyfriend. And the
screw comes round and gives you, like, 15 letters and you just
think 'Oh no'. But I got a lot of good-natured teasing – other
women being interested in who's written to you and being
really pleased for you – and I don't know that I would be that
generous under the same conditions.

Martha

This response was one experienced by all the Greenham women I
spoke to:

Mary   How did the other women react to you?
Barbara   Well, they thought it was awful, that sentence that I
            got just for cutting a hole in a fence. I think the
            embarrassing thing was getting more letters and
            flowers and stuff which they didn't get. Every post
            there would be masses of letters, every week. I nev-
            er had a time when I didn't have flowers in my cell.
            That was the embarrassing bit really, although it

> was nice for me, I mean it was lovely for me because
> you had all that support to keep you going, but for
> other women, when they never had a letter.
> *Mary*   But they didn't show resentment at that?
> *Barbara* No, no.

Even so, while the women experienced no direct expressions
of resentment, there were prisoners whose situation was made
worse by the presence of the Greenham women. One woman
tells how she and others were moved out of Holloway, down
to Pucklechurch, near Bristol, to make space for the peace
campaigners.

> *Collette*   I think the Pucklechurch thing will stick with me as
> the bitterest thing with the slop out, potties, washing
> in cold water, being away from London. They were
> getting all their privileges. They would walk on the
> landings and say 'Well I choose to be here'. They
> were all quite demanding, they commanded a lot of
> attention and the press were outside and they were
> in newspapers every day.
> *Mary*   Was there any hostility to them?
> *Collette*   No, I don't think so because they were all women
> lovers and peace lovers. No, I don't think so.

Prison officers' attempts to orchestrate resentment depended for
their success on the acceptability of the target. The Greenham
women were not drawn from that group of already marginalized
women. Most of them were from the articulate middle classes and
thus likely to be given status in a situation which exaggerates social
hierarchies. Another middle-class prisoner, a doctor convicted of
kidnapping, recognized this in her own experience of prison.

> The staff didn't know how to treat me, the staff and the kids,
> they never do when they get someone who is out of the run.
> They pretended to treat you just like everybody else and then
> proceeded not to. I played chess with the governor once a
> week which was nice. When somebody of education and sta-
> tus goes into prison, nobody knows how to treat them.
> *Beatrice*

The Greenham women also managed to combat, in prison, the
mass media depictions of them as 'folk devils'. As lively, per-
sonable, confident women who challenged the system they com-
manded interest and respect. Furthermore, they were organized to

subvert the disciplinary regime of the prison. These women were not isolated. The daily letters and deliveries of flowers were a continual reminder of their connection with others in the world outside. For them prison was not an exclusion, they remained part of their former community. Their model of femininity may have posed a problem for the tabloid press (see Cook and Kirk 1983) but it was a model with a recognized pedigree. Women who suffer on behalf of others are the stuff of heroines from Joan of Arc to Odette. Moreover, they are women who choose, who act in full awareness, who are clear about their own concerns. While even these women found their autonomy and self-direction threatened and inhibited by the prison regime (see Barbara, p. 43, and Judith p. 41, 43), they were not easily excluded or demoted down the hierarchy by prison officers.

Those who were successfully targeted for exclusion were those whose place in society was already marginal – the personally weak, with few resources, and those accused of crimes that are seen to be beyond the pale. Defining these women as outcasts allows others to redefine themselves as less excluded, indeed as included in the social body which condemns the ultimate outcast. Thus the hierarchy of prisoners upholds the hierarchy of prison authority, and the status pattern of the outside world. By withdrawing and retaliating, women are incorporated within the life of the prison and incorporation involves the reproduction of the world of the prison. So all-embracing is this world that there is little space in which an active and oppositional sense of self can develop. However, there is one further mode of adaptation to prison life which at the same time activates and denies the self.

4 Self-mutilation

The incidence of self-mutilation by women prisoners has been the subject of much comment (cf. Heidensohn 1985: 73; Dobash et al. 1986: 153; O'Dwyer, et al. 1987: 182). This practice appears to be a response to an intolerable situation and a response found more usually among women.

Women turn their frustration and anger inwards. Self-mutilation is now a major problem among women prisoners. Self-mutilation involves anything from striking a cut in the forearm, to pulling out an eye. Home Office figures show that

while less than one out of every 100 men mutilate themselves
in prison, the same figure for women is *one in six*.

> (Benn and Tchaikovsky 1987; emphasis in original)

Only one of the 34 women interviewed discussed her own self-
mutilation, inflicted in an attempt to make others aware of her
distress and so bring about a change of circumstances.

Mandy	I did one [mutilation] when I was in prison. That was because I was so depressed with where I was situated. I didn't like the wing I was put on because I felt under threat. I just wanted to do something to get out of it. That was with a broken toothbrush, breaking the toothbrush and driving it up my arm.
Mary	What happened when you did that?
Mandy	Not a lot, they just didn't want to know. It didn't need stitching so they just left it.

Here, in an inverted form of control, the woman seeks to take
some power to herself by inflicting on herself a pain greater than
that inflicted by others on her. In injuring and mutilating herself
she, at one and the same time, denies herself and yet wields power,
if only over herself.

> I just felt so helpless, powerless, that the only way I could sort
> of get back the power was to slash at myself, mutilate my own
> body.
>
> (quoted in Evans 1991)

Others had witnessed the process, or the aftermath, and they
chronicled the indifference and hostility with which such actions
were met:

> A lot of girls on C wing cut their arms up, cut their bodies up. I
> don't think I've seen so much blood and scars. They mutilated
> their bodies. They were frustrated. And all you heard the
> officer say was 'Oh dear she's attempting, she's seeking atten-
> tion again'. I said 'I don't believe you people'. I used to say
> 'Well you're women too, don't you understand?' And they
> walk around with their keys, they were so key happy. They
> looked at you as if you were just the scum of the earth. I used
> to say 'There must be somebody out there that you love and
> would you treat them the way you treat us?'
>
> *Bella*

Women who seriously damage themselves or their surroundings are often confined to the strips. 'They are held in cells with no furniture and they are allowed only a canvas, or tough nylon, shift to wear' (Stevenson 1989: 15). Those whose injuries require sutures may be given treatment without anaesthetic (O'Dwyer and Carlen 1985: 171). The institutional response is punitive, the pain is denied and the perpetrator is further punished. By solitary confinement she is further denied control over her own person. The response of the prison is a further negation of the self. For some women this may mean a removal from prison to a special hospital, with no release date.

It is not surprising that some women respond to such negation with the ultimate self-injury of death. The final act of the self is the destruction of the self. Such a suicide may be the result of an injury ignored, or the result of indifference displayed by the authorities in ignoring the cry for help, or it may be the last decision taken by the denied self. Bella was aware of the danger to her friend. She tried to alert the nurses in Broadmoor but to no effect.

I met a girl in prison called Christine. We became good friends. I stopped her committing suicide three times in prison. Then this time I just felt that she was going to do it. She said 'I don't feel well, you're OK now?' I said 'Yes, I'm OK Christine, but why are you saying am I OK?' 'I just want to know that you're alright'. And I knew that she was going. I went in the office and said 'Please do something for Christine' and they kicked me out of the office and told me to go to work and stop the noise, they wanted to do their handover. She hung herself.

Self-injury and suicide are the acts of the self turned against the self. Such actions say much for the conditions from which they spring, and the pain engendered by those conditions.

However, even with her own death the prisoner is denied. Speaking of a woman who burnt to death in her cell when the alarm bell had been immobilized, Fran said:

She was disappeared, the card was taken off the door and it was as though she had never existed.

Appalled by the lack of recognition of a life and a death, Fran organized a collection among the women prisoners and arranged for a large bunch of flowers to be delivered to the prison. She had discussed with the governor a plan to put the flowers in the chapel and have a focus for remembering the dead woman. However, when the flowers were delivered they were divided into numerous small vases and distributed about the prison. The governor was away and, Fran was told, her deputy feared that any recognition of the death might provoke a riot.

Death is the woman's ultimate act but she is not allowed to own that act. Her death is unmarked. Even after she becomes a body she becomes a nobody. And other prisoners witness that neither her existence nor her non-existence is recognized. Thus their own worth is announced.

The structural preconditions for subjective change exist within prisons. They are to be found in any total institution (Goffman 1987) in which the inmate is to be transformed from a former self to a new self which better fits the institution. The woman prisoner is removed from familiar surroundings that evoke customary responses. She is placed in a strange situation in which her ability to decide, to structure her responses, is denied. She is subject to arbitrary rule enforcement and Draconian discipline. She is fearful and confused. She is clearly not who she was, she does not know who she is nor who she will become. She needs to find a way of reacting appropriately in a hostile environment. Whatever the response, it is an adaptation to that environment. In adapting she is changed. How will such change affect her in the outside world? How easily can she adapt again to life beyond prison?

4
GETTING OUT – BUT NOT GETTING AWAY

It's like expecting an alien to come down from a totally different planet – because that's what prison is like. There you're in an environment that's not real – you're separated from the rest of society. So you come out and you just don't know what to do. And that's when you go back to knowing what you know is safe – which is usually crime.

Linda

Prison does distort your thinking incredibly. Everything is distorted so completely. People find it hard to catch what it is about prison that is so destructive, but it is also what you bring out with you.

Fran

Within the prison each woman is closed off from the wider society and held within the narrow world of the prison. Placed by others, she has no space in which to define herself. She returns to society disorientated and disempowered. For her the choice seems to lie between returning to a former way of life or going nowhere. This is the dilemma articulated by Linda and Fran. This was Alice's experience. It is the experience of many.

Women described themselves as changed by prison. With reception began a process by which each woman was taken out and taken down. Excluded from society, she was stripped of all her possessions, of her dignity, of her identity. She had less, she was made less. She was placed and held beyond responsibility, denied the authority to act on her own behalf or on behalf of others.

Dismissed, degraded and denied, she was subject to a regime
which demands docility. Her skills were unused. Her new role was
characterized by ineffectiveness.

Yet on release a woman is faced with a series of demands. She is
expected to be effective in a world from which she has been
estranged. She must find a home, obtain a job or a source of
income, establish or re-establish personal relationships. For some
women, retrieving their children from care is a primary goal, but it
is one that is dependent on finding a home. Finding a job presents
the woman with the dilemma of whether or not to declare her
criminal conviction. Whatever disadvantages the woman suffered
from before prison she now faces the world with the added disadvantage of a prison experience and a prison record. She is a prisoner and she brings this knowledge, this identity, out into the
world. The prison experience will affect her response to the outside world, the prison record will affect the response of others to
her. When she comes out she brings something of the prison with
her – something more lasting than the small discharge grant.[1] As
Fran put it:

You can never leave prison, because prison never leaves you.

Facing the world

Although the effects of prison may vary from woman to woman,
there was a consistent reiteration of the disorientation which
women experienced on leaving prison. Out of prison, they felt out
of place. Prison had so effectively socialized the women into the
regime that the outside world was strange and unaccommodating.
Women spoke of their fear on first leaving prison. Susan had a
place in bed and breakfast accommodation where she felt lonely
and bewildered. Like so many of the women, Susan brought out
with her the incompetence and low self-esteem that she had
learned in prison. A former white-collar criminal with the social
skills consistent with her job and the organizational skills consistent with her crime, Susan, on first leaving prison, lacked the confidence to leave her bedsitter. She was unable to move into the
world to which she was returned. She brought the prison out with
her and continued to be imprisoned.

I sat there and I thought 'Well I'm more alone here than I
ever was in prison'. I had nobody to talk to and I was too
frightened to go out – and I really wished I was back inside.

Again and again, women chronicled their feelings of misplacement:

> That first day, when I was released, I thought I was OK. I thought I could cope with whatever the world threw at me. And at the end of the very first day, I was a broken pathetic specimen. I didn't know where to start, who to go to, where to turn.
>
> *Cara*

> The awful panic feelings that you're no good, you're useless – you were looking forward, you were going out into this world and it was going to be so wonderful and then you come out. It's not. And you felt so useless and hopeless and worthless.
>
> *Meg*

Excluded and degraded by the prison, taken out and taken down, many women felt that they were still apart from the rest of society. Yet, although apart, they felt that they were subject to the gaze and judgement of others. The effect of constant surveillance continues as this aspect, too, of prison life is brought out with the women.

> I really felt like an outsider. I also felt I had 'criminal' tattooed on my forehead, for the whole world to see. And I was very self-conscious. I had no confidence in myself at all. The whole world was just horrible, even crossing the road was difficult.
>
> *Cara*

> The awful gut feeling that I'd experienced after being released from prison. Just getting on a bus – you know the bus is going in the right direction, you know you're getting on the right bus, but you get on and you think 'Oh my God, can I get the money right?' And it's the same wherever you go. In the supermarket if you're being held up you think 'Oh I'm holding everyone up. Everyone can see.' 'Is this woman from prison? Can she do it?'
>
> *Meg*

Thus, dislocated and disempowered, the woman ex-prisoner has to set about making a place for herself.

Facing the family

For some women the immediate problem on leaving prison is to re-establish a relationship with their children, and with other members of their family. Prison had not only separated these women from their children but also, in many cases, engendered doubts as to their ability to relate to the children. The prison continued to structure the mothers' experience. Many had lost the place they had once had in their children's lives. Paula wondered if she occupied any place at all, if she had any reality for her children.

> I was talking to the children in a very funny sort of way because I wondered when I'd spoken to them if they heard me – the fact that I was in prison. We're talking now about a 10-year-old girl, a 17-year-old young man and a 15-year-old young man who had been living by themselves actually for a year. So I was embarrassed when I spoke to them in case they thought: 'Well you come out of prison, how dare you tell me.'

Cara found that her child no longer saw her as her mother:

> There she was – two and a half, chatting away with her own little personality, not at all a baby, an 18-month-old baby that I'd left behind. My mum was her mum, if she was upset or hurt herself she just went straight to my mum.

Many women suffered rejection by members of their family. The prison continued to separate and distort the perspective:

> I don't have three brothers now, I have one. It's annihilated two brothers. It might as well have taken them and shot them – and not only them but it's taken their children.
>
> *Sandy*

> My eldest son doesn't have anything to do with me because – oh he thought it was awful. It broke up my family.
>
> *Doris*

This rejection and exclusion could extend to anyone who continued to be allied with or to support the ex-prisoner:

> The majority of my family stopped speaking to even my mother when I was in prison – wanted nothing to do with it.
>
> *Paula*

Finding a place

The prison past also influences the present in relation to employment. The Rehabilitation of Offenders Act 1974 allows for the 'spending' of convictions after a given period. This means that for the majority of jobs, the ex-prisoner need not declare her conviction. The 'given period', however, varies with the length of the sentence. All sentences of more than two and a half years are never spent, those of between six months and two and a half years are 'spent' after ten years, while for those of less than six months the period is seven years (Treverton-Jones 1989). But, this still means that, on leaving prison, the woman must declare her conviction to a future employer, or risk dismissal (and further prosecution) should the conviction subsequently be discovered. Speaking of herself and her husband, Bernice articulates the problem:

> You just want to be like the rest, but there's that whole thing of hoping you don't have to keep proving yourself. All the time both of us have to lie, have to say we don't have criminal records. We live through hell, thinking 'Are they going to find out?'

Yet to declare the prison record is to invite rejection or greater control. On leaving prison, Bernice was anxious to put her experience to good use by moving from teaching to social work.

> I applied for jobs, social working type jobs, which I felt I was well qualified to do, especially having been in prison. And every job I applied for I got shortlisted for. There'd be four or five people on the interview panel and three people you could see were very interested and two people you could see, immediately you got in there you knew you wouldn't get the job. I went to about half a dozen interviews. I wanted so badly to be able to use it. I really felt I was in a position to do good work, to make something of it.

Currently both she and her husband are working in this area, but neither has declared the prison past.

Those who are honest in admitting to their criminal record find themselves subject to further surveillance. Barbara, a Greenham woman, was a vicar's wife. Without a prison sentence it is unlikely that she would have been questioned about her political activities in applying for jobs:

> I had a job as a manager of a charity shop. They said 'It's alright as long as she doesn't use the shop for peace activities' – as if I was going to set it up as a peace shop. I think that's quite odd in a way, that people think they need to, because of that they have some kind of control over me.

> Another one was a family aide, it was a part-time job. Again
> the woman there said 'Of course I have to say this but we
> would expect that you wouldn't talk about CND'. I think she
> meant with the people I had to go and visit. I mean it's really
> odd, isn't it. They feel they have to do this. I think it's power, I
> think they must have a kind of knowledge about you.

As Barbara realizes, to admit that she has been to prison is to
invite further interrogation and control. It is to allow the public to
perpetuate the sentence by considering it appropriate to treat ex-
prisoners differently from other women. Official punishment is no
longer publicly executed but there is a persistence of public
punishment in the punitive attitudes and intrusive behaviour that
the women encountered. The boundaries of their existence continued to be defined by others in a way which denied them the
space to construct their own responses. They were both pushed out
by unacceptance, and pulled in by interrogation and vigilance.

Paula describes an exchange with a shopkeeper who had no
grounds to doubt her creditworthiness:

> There was a butcher's shop in the marketplace where I nor-
> mally purchased my stuff. Every month I'd get a large amount
> of meat and pay by cheque. I'd tell him what I wanted, he'd
> pack it and send it round. And this particular day I went to
> purchase the meat and he said to me 'I can't accept your
> cheque, I hear you were in prison, is it true?' And I remember
> looking at him and wanting to curse him, to say 'How dare
> you assume that I went to prison for stealing?' Because in my
> own mind I know I can't steal. I walked out.

Such stigmatization of ex-prisoners extends throughout society.
Fran describes her interview at an Oxbridge college where she
was seen primarily as an ex-prisoner, and as a stereotypical ex-
prisoner, rather than as a future student:

> They said things like 'Would you sign to say that you wouldn't
> deal drugs around campus?' I said 'I've never dealt drugs in
> my life so why should I start now?' My back was up, I was very
> angry. They made me feel such rubbish. They asked me what
> Dickens I'd read, so I told them, *Little Dorrit*, and they said
> 'Oh I suppose you read that because it was based in a prison
> and you have an affinity with it.' I thought 'Oh Christ, leave
> me alone, I just want to be educated'.

Others found that admitting to a criminal record can change the responses of classmates. Once again the 'ex-prisoner' label dominates and distorts future interaction. Laura found that she had to deal not only with the impact of prison on her life, but with the reaction of others to that knowledge, and with her interpretation of that reaction:

> I was all for being honest, but of course being honest around people who maybe didn't have any concept of a criminal life. I was back on my college course trying my best to catch up, and also cope with maybe what they were thinking. And I did actually get a bit self-conscious about it. [I thought] 'Those people actually think I'm an out-and-out criminal. They probably think that I'm going to rob them now. They'll watch their bags'.

For some women the world of the prison is recreated outside the prison by other ex-prisoners. Terri suffered a double exclusion, both inside and after prison. Since her offence involved the death of her child, she had spent her time in prison segregated from other prisoners under Rule 43. On leaving prison she had moved into a hostel for ex-offenders but her probation officer had advised her to keep her offence secret and to tell the other residents that she had been convicted of fraud. This Terri agreed to do.

> In prison there is a pecking order and Rule 43s are right at the bottom and a lot of people, when they come out, especially where I'm living, have this prison mentality. Some people are better than others even though they have all been inside.

As inside the prison, so outside the prison, those who themselves are controlled by the system become part of that system in controlling others. Hierarchies are reproduced and the status quo is preserved.

Media images

Each of the women that I interviewed was aware that her status as an ex-prisoner gave her an identity, in the eyes of others, over which she had little control. Many found that this one aspect of their biography dominated all others once it became public. Thus shoppers became the object of suspicion, employees were subject to excessive surveillance, and students felt vulnerable and caricatured if they admitted to their prison past. The women were conscious of the ways in which their lives were being understood in the context of dominant images of prisoners and ex-prisoners. Many were aware that such images are continuously constructed by the mass media. Some had personal experience of the way in which individual experience is placed within a framework which stereotypes.

A worker in a voluntary sector organization frequently used by journalists articulated the problem. Despite her university education and her ten years' experience of project work and campaigning, her prison past is always prioritized by the mass media. Furthermore, she is expected to provide narrative description rather than analytic comment.

> The assumption there is that your expertise is only because you lived in prison. There is an assumption that you must be thick, you must be stupid and you're not going to have any other knowledge.
>
> *Fran*

The status of a subject is communicated usually by the place the subject occupies in the mass media representation. It is Fran's experience that ex-prisoners are given no space of their own, a practice which both confirms their low status and reiterates their 'outsider' identity.

> The ex-prisoner – the human interest bit – is established walking through a park or on a pavement, or in an open setting. If you are an expert usually you are 'established' in your office, or in your own home.
>
> *Fran*

The dominance of the media framework in the presentation of material to the public was apparent in the personal experience of two other women. Barbara had been approached by researchers for a BBC radio programme who wanted to do something on her prison experience. However, while Barbara wanted to use the programme to talk about a fellow prisoner who had died in custody, the programme makers wanted to use Barbara's position as a vicar's wife as the focus of interest.

> It's quite difficult to control the media, what you want to say and what they want to say. There was a *Woman's Hour* programme and I wanted to talk about this woman who died, and he wanted to record people going into church and asking them

about what they felt about me. I thought 'No way, I'm not agreeing to that'.

Barbara, as an ex-prisoner, was expected to be the subject of comment by others; she was not expected to be the author of comment on her own experience. The disempowerment of prison continues.

Meg's experience of the mass media is an illustration not only of the way ex-prisoners are stereotyped but also of the perpetuation of stigma. Meg left prison after serving ten years of a life sentence. She had returned to her former neighbourhood and had not changed her name or made any attempt to hide her identity. Nor had she discussed her past with her new neighbours in the block of flats in which she lived. One morning she was surprised by the local press:

> There was a knock on the door – half past eight in the morning – I opened it and a man stood there with a board in his hand. And he said 'Mrs Murray?' As I said 'Yes' a photographer leapt from behind the wall and flashed a camera at me. Of course I was [looking startled]. It was the newspapers. And I had half an hour's fight with them. In fact he put his foot in the door. He tried to push the door open with his elbow. I slammed that door so hard. There was what seemed like a mad man kicking this door. And I said 'You're not allowed to do that' [looking angry] and as I did that he took another one and, of course, that was the one in the newspaper – there's this aggressive woman.

Fortunately for Meg, her family gave her support through the ordeal of publication, and her new neighbours expressed sympathetic concern. The media presentation did not undermine the positive impression they had formed of her. However, such presentations do serve to support existing images of the woman criminal and ex-prisoner. They encourage the typifications of people and experience which underlie the responses encountered by other women as they try to live in the community as ex-prisoners. In discussing their experience the women articulated the twin dilemmas of the ex-prisoner: secrecy and surveillance. To deny the past is to collude in the shame, to accept the status of an outsider with a guilty and unredeemable secret. To admit to the past is to invite mistrust, to give others further power to block access to new jobs, new relationships – a new way of life. With a knowledge of their past, others would subject these women to greater surveillance. Living with a secret involves feelings of deceit and unease at the fear of exposure. A declaration of her record renders the woman vulnerable to continued scrutiny of and intrusion into her life. She is subject to greater control by others: her own attempts at greater autonomy and self-direction are frustrated. She is placed by others and has difficulty in finding her own place. It is the prevalence of such responses that made many women feel the need for a space in which their situation was understood and their individuality recognized. Groups run by and for ex-prisoners provide such a space.

Being with ex-prisoners: finding a space

Of the 34 women I interviewed over half were, or had been, involved with one of the ex-prisoner organizations for women. Seven of the women were paid workers in such an organization. This high proportion is, of course, due to my method of selection (see Appendix 1). Three organizations are considered here:
Women In Prison (WIP) was established in October 1983 as a campaigning and support group run by ex-prisoners.

> We felt there was a need for an ex-prisoner pressure group committed to effecting real change within the prison system. By listening to and gathering evidence directly from prisoners and ex-prisoners, and by making their experiences known, we hope to change people's attitudes towards imprisonment.
> (Women In Prison 1987: 1)

For a fuller account see Carlen and Tchaikovsky (1985).
Women in Special Hospitals (WISH) was established in 1990 by a former worker from WIP and other concerned women. WISH extends the work of WIP into the special hospitals, regional secure units and prison psychiatric units. WISH gives a voice to the many forgotten and neglected women who live there.
The Creative And Supportive Trust (CAST) was established in 1981 by an ex-prisoner with the help of the Education Department of Holloway Prison. CAST offers support and facilities to women coming out of prison, in order that they might develop the creative, social and technical skills which will help them in building a new life. For a fuller account see Hicks and Carlen (1985: 136); and Carlen (1990: 100–2).
These organizations provide a distinctive service for women trying to make a new life for themselves. As women-only organizations, they give women the opportunity of discovering their

strengths as women, rather than working under the direction and gaze of men. As ex-prisoner organizations they provide a space in which the difficulties of the woman ex-prisoner are understood and can be addressed.

Meg draws on her own experience in recognizing the needs of the women who come to CAST:

> The one thing that everyone lacks coming out of prison, no matter how long they served, is confidence. It is completely gone – they just can't do anything. And we've had a few that we've put into different places and colleges and they come running back [saying] 'I don't fit in'. And it's because they can't be honest. They feel that they are still on their own, and they feel that they are totally alien, that they are different. When anyone comes out of prison there is a certain length of time when people feel like that and it's getting them through that period. And you do feel different. I know exactly what they feel like. I know exactly what they mean.

This strong identification allows Meg to meet the immediate needs of the women and to provide a context in which they are neither patronized nor infantalized.

> And they know that they can run back here whenever they are hurting, as well as coming in and learning skills. Occasionally I'll get a phone call, 'Oh Meg I want to come in and do photography but I haven't got the bus fare'. We do pay fares, or I'll go and meet them. If they were in a college they couldn't do that, (a) their pride wouldn't let them and (b) that would make them different from everyone else. Whereas here they know they can say that and nobody will take any notice.

Believing in the potential of the women, Meg encourages them to relate to her as an equal, to see themselves as they see her.

> They still come and say 'Can't believe you've been in prison, you're just not the sort'. And I say 'OK why do you say that? To me you don't look the sort, so why were you there? Why throw your life away? Why stamp yourself? Why say to yourself "Well, I'm the sort who should go but she's not the sort who should go?" Why don't you think to yourself "Well, I shouldn't go either?" '

For many who use the project, CAST is experienced as uniquely suited to their needs. Laura was initially placed at CAST on a

community service order. There she felt secure enough to con-
template changing her lifestyle:

> I felt I don't need this criminal thing in my life. I've got ex-
> criminals around me now. It's like fitting in. This was like a
> kind of middle ground for me. It was new and people who had
> come from prison too, and we all had similar attitudes. I just
> felt good there and although I'd finished my community ser-
> vice order, I carried on going to CAST.

For Laura the sense of belonging experienced at CAST was a
contrast with the sense of difference which she had experienced at
a local college (see p. 61).

> I came to the conclusion that if I'd known about CAST when I
> was in prison it would have been much better for me. It would
> have been the stepping stone I needed because going straight
> into college coming from prison, and especially getting nicked
> again during the college course, it was all this stigma business.
> Like I say, fitting in.

Again and again those who talked about the organizations run
by ex-prisoners stressed a sense of belonging resulting from a
shared prison experience. Using metaphors of transition (for
example, stepping stones, bridge) they also expressed a sense
of progress. Like other workers in this area, Judith, from WIP,
contrasts her approach to ex-prisoners, based on empathy, with
that of the professional dependent on formal training.

> It would take you hours to try to explain that feeling that it
> gives you, when someone rattles the keys or when you hear a
> door slam. You turn around just to make sure that it's not
> shutting behind you, it's just being able to connect with how
> somebody feels. Until you know what it feels like, not to know
> exactly when you're going, and have them playing around and
> winding up and not telling you what day you're going to be
> released etcetera, you will never really know what it's like.
> And because you do know, and you are working with other
> people who have been in the same situation you have been in,
> you can help. They know you are not just an interfering social
> worker. That breaks down a lot of the initial barriers and
> allows you to work with the person and not with the act that
> they put on. Paula put it the best way, her job as welfare
> worker is building bridges between the state and the women,
> so that the women get everything they are entitled to. Build-

ing bridges, that's what it is. Building bridges between people and society again. And to be able to do that is good.

The ex-prisoners running these organizations are able to draw on important shared experiences when working with the women who attend the projects. This emphasis on similarity does much to counteract the feelings of difference, stigma and exclusion which women ex-prisoners encounter elsewhere. Women are encouraged to see themselves as capable of moving through present difficulties, as the workers and other clients have done. Meg described the informal sessions which take place in addition to the provision of classes at CAST.

What most of them haven't got is families to guide them in any direction. So we all sit down there, like a family, and it's amazing what comes out. And they know they can come in here, and even if they have felt that they're slipping back they know they can come in here and talk quite honestly about it. One came in here and I said 'OK let's look at it. If you do that you end up in a van going back to Holloway. If you don't where can we go from there?'

Women are encouraged to be active agents, with others, in the overcoming of difficulties. They are encouraged to take responsibility and find direction in their lives. For those who work for the empowerment of others the prison experience becomes a resource to be drawn on. However, working in this way, is not only satisfying but also extremely demanding since the prison experience is continually relived. Paula, at WIP, discusses this:

When I go and visit a woman that's just been sentenced, and I'm talking to her, I can feel every single bit of my first day in prison coming back to me. And in the first three or four visits I actually share my experience with her. I don't tell her about myself, but emotionally I'm sharing that experience because I can feel the pain. I wouldn't want to stop working with these women but as long as I'm working with them, I'll always remember myself.

The empathy which makes her an effective worker also makes her vulnerable:

I've been here now three and a half years – ex-prisoners can be quite damaging – you want so much to do things for people in prison that you wanted done for yourself when you were there. And you want to do it all. And you cannot do it all and you have to share it, and you also have to have a barrier where you cut off, and I suppose the fact that I am an ex-prisoner [means] I never know where to cut off.

Being with ex-prisoners, as an ex-prisoner, is for many women an important part of the successful transition from prison to the wider society. However, unless it is a transition, the women may find themselves still involved in an area of life that was not, initially, their choice.

One thing that has bothered me is that one is still hanging in on prison. Is it because we just can't leave that field?

Kathy

There is an irony in the fact that those who are most effective in facilitating the transition of others may feel themselves to be trapped in the identity of ex-prisoner. Moving out from the prison is not easy. Much of the prison goes with the woman, constraining her choices, constructing her responses. Dislocated and disempowered by the prison experience, each woman needs a space in which she can construct a sense of an autonomous self, one which relates to others and acts on their and her own behalf. For many women the only available space is that from which she was removed. Even this raises problems. Because of their prison identity, some women felt out of place in their former environment. For others, a return to a former way of life meant a return to crime and the likelihood of a return to prison.

Imprisonment is, for many women, the continuation of a process of marginalization and exclusion. The factors which initially contributed to this process continue to operate, now aggravated by the experience of prison. There continue to be structural blocks to positive subjective change in the lives of the women. These are experienced in four areas.

1 Housing
2 Labour market and educational provision
3 Social Services
4 Health

1 *Housing*

Recent research has highlighted the accommodation problems faced by women leaving prison (Wilkinson 1988; Carlen 1990).

This is not a problem unique to ex-prisoners. It is an area in which women are under-resourced both as tenants and as homeowners (Austerberry and Watson 1983). Many women have experienced homelessness or insecure accommodation prior to prison (Wilkinson 1988). However, imprisonment may have resulted in the loss of a home when mortgage payments ceased to be made or tenancies were lost through rent arrears. Although there is provision to meet the rent of those imprisoned for less than a year, and those imprisoned for longer may agree to give up the tenancy on condition that they are rehoused on release, many women are unaware or unclear of their rights in this area.

> Social pay your rent for a year, after that they'll take your tenancy, but in that time you write to them and say 'I want to relinquish the tenancy on the understanding I'm rehoused'. Get that agreement and then they've got to rehouse you when you come out. So many women have their properties taken and then they're put in halfway houses, bed and breakfasts, simply because they don't know.
>
> *Lisa*

However, those who are rehoused are likely to find themselves living in 'difficult-to-let' properties in areas with a high rate of burglary and property theft. Apart from the obvious dangers and disadvantages of this situation, the ex-prisoner also faces difficulties in finding an insurance company to cover her for loss of personal property or household contents. Most companies refuse such cover without considering the circumstances of the woman or the crime.

Many women are made homeless by their prison experience. Other women may come out of prison to find their homes have been squatted, burgled, vandalized or damaged in other ways.

> I used to sit in prison and picture this place. I knew we'd been burgled. I knew there'd been a flood which brought down this ceiling and that ceiling.
>
> *Carole*

A satisfactory dwelling place is not only essential for the woman's health and safety, it is also necessary if she is to obtain parole. However, while a parole board requires an acceptable address before assigning a release date, many hostels will not give a place until the woman has a definite release date. In such circumstances many women are forced to return to unsatisfactory or violent relationships in order to supply the necessary address.

Any woman trying to find a home, without an above average income, will find herself disadvantaged by recent legislation on housing. The right to buy council property, which was conferred by the 1980 Housing Act, has resulted in a reduction in the amount of rented accommodation in the public sector. Central government has consistently opposed attempts by local councils to improve the situation. Those which sought to use the rates in this way were threatened with a loss of government grant (Carlen 1990: 66–7). The situation has been worsened by the 1985 Housing Act's definition of local authorities' responsibilities for homeless people. Only those 'in priority need' have the right to be given a permanent home. This means women with dependent children, or pregnant women, or those considered to be 'vulnerable', perhaps for health reasons. The ex-prisoner, however, may find difficulty in proving a local connection with the area in which she wishes to be housed. Some women may in fact wish to move away from former localities in order to escape from the influences that led to imprisonment. Some may have lived in a number of areas, on a temporary basis, prior to imprisonment. Even if a woman can prove a local connection she needs also to show that she was not intentionally homeless, that is, that she had not previously given up a home or lost it through eviction. Once again a chaotic lifestyle, or poverty, continue to put the woman at a disadvantage. The effect of the legislation is to make it even more difficult for her to change her life.

Without a claim to priority need, a woman faces the options of temporary accommodation in a bed and breakfast hostel, or finding a place in a housing project or a hostel provided by the voluntary sector. Many women prefer women-only accommodation. For some this is the only way to feel safe after a history of abuse by men; others express a need for some time to themselves before becoming involved in relationships with men (Carlen 1990: 45; HM Inspectorate of Probation 1991: para 4.5.1). Even if they aim to provide a balance of the sexes, mixed hostels usually have a far higher proportion of men than women, since there are more men than women competing for places and grant funders may require evidence of full usage if the grant is to be maintained (Carlen 1990: 46). The result is that the few women in such a hostel would be far outnumbered and would probably feel uncomfortable and unsafe. Similarly, the small numbers of women ex-prisoners seeking accommodation nationally works against the adequate provision of women-only hostels. It is only in the large urban conurbations that such hostels are to be found. In other areas the smaller numbers of women make the project economically unviable. Once again women are marginalized by structures designed in response to financial constraint rather than social need. Once again women who have been vulnerable to abuse by men are likely to find themselves in a situation where such abuse is likely to recur.

2 *Labour market and educational provision*

The women who go to prison are usually among the most disadvantaged in terms of educational and vocational training. Poverty pervades their lives (Carlen 1988). Frequently a history of truancy from school has been followed by unemployment or casual low-paid work. This situation has caused some commentators to call for the prison authorities to use the sentenced time 'to enhance their skills and halt the downward spiral' (Women's National Commission 1991: 26). However, while women may gain much from education in terms of self-esteem, confidence and self-knowledge, the experience is unlikely to affect their position in the labour market. As Christine Wilkinson (1988) has argued, it is their position as women within the social structure, rather than their inadequacy as individuals, which accounts for their poverty and unemployment. As mothers of young children, many were unable to find, or could not afford, child care to enable them to work full-time. The part-time work available to them, for example in catering and cleaning, was usually so poorly paid that it was not worth taking. Even those without children, or with child-care provision, are likely to find themselves marginalized by the sexual division of labour. Despite the provisions of the 1975 Sex Discrimination Act, men's jobs and women's jobs continue to be segregated both horizontally (into different occupations) and vertically (with women occupying subordinate positions within the same occupation) (Walby 1990; Grint 1991). The jobs which women may reasonably expect to get are those concentrated in the lower-paid areas of the manufacturing and the service sector. Since the 1975 Equal Pay Act applies only to men and women doing the same job it has had little effect on the wages gap. In 1990 women on average earned 63.1 per cent of men's hourly rate and ten years after the implementation of the Equal Pay Act there had been an improvement of only 10 per cent (Walby 1990: 51). In 1986 women earned 74 per cent of men's hourly rate, or 66 per cent of men's gross weekly earnings since men have greater access to shift work and overtime (Walby 1990: 25). For part-time workers the gap is greater. These women, who constituted 44 per cent of the female workforce in 1986, earned only 56 per cent of men's hourly rate or 76 per cent of women's full-time hourly rate (Walby 1990: 25, 54). Part-time workers are further disadvantaged by greater job insecurity and they do not qualify for many of the benefits accruing to full-time employment.

The current recession has also affected women's employment. Although employment for women, particularly part-time employment, has risen in recent years, the proportion of women who are unemployed is similar to that for men. For 1984–6 the rate for women was 10 per cent and for men it was 11 per cent (*Employment Gazette*, March 1988: 172, cited in Walby 1990: 25). This situation is aggravated by racism – for black men in the same period the unemployment rate was 21 per cent and for black women it was 19 per cent (Walby 1990: 45).

Disadvantaged as women in the labour market, the status of ex-prisoner makes the situation even worse. The experiences of many of the women I interviewed confirmed the findings of Wilkinson (1988: 168). The surest way to obtain employment was to conceal the prison record, and thus risk further exclusion if discovered.

For some women, like Kathy and Hazel, prison provided an introduction to education. This was something they wished to pursue on leaving prison. Education can be an experience in which time for reflection and the acquisition of new skills lead to a change in self-perception and a growth in confidence in dealing with others. However, recent changes in funding policies by central and local governments pose a threat to all adult education and especially to the types of courses needed by those with little experience of the education system. Labour councils fearing community charge capping, and Conservative councils wishing to impose a low community charge, look for areas of possible economy. While there is a statutory obligation to provide education for five- to 16-year-olds there is no such obligation on the provision of adult education. This has resulted in the underfunding or in some cases the withdrawal of public funds from adult education (Hull and Coben 1991: 11). For example, in the London Borough of Islington a cut of 1 per cent in schools was achieved by cutting adult education by 20 per cent (Payne 1991a: 9).

The White Paper on adult education, *Education and Training for the 21st Century* (Department of Education and Science/Employment Department Group 1991), is expected to have an impact on the types of courses provided. It is the government's intention to charge full fees for all courses which are not work-related or certificate-bearing. This discourages the provision of courses which focus on self-development and provide a space in which students explore their potential before undertaking a vocational or academic course. It certainly puts such courses beyond the means of the poor and the poorly educated who most need them.

3 *Social services*

Women leaving prison are likely to encounter the DSS in two contexts: as a source of income and as the official caretakers of their children. In both contexts they are likely to be experienced by the women as a block to rather than as a facilitator of change.

Welfare provision in the United Kingdom is based on the ideologically dominant model of the family in which a male bread-winner provides for a financially dependent wife and children. As this arrangement is to be found in only a minority of families, the majority of adult women (82 per cent) are disadvantaged in their entitlement to social security payments (Callender 1987; Millar and Glendinning 1987). Many women have histories of limited or discontinuous employment, coupled with sole responsibility for child care; they can expect lower levels of benefit than men. Millar and Glendinning (1987: 25) argue that 'the ideology of dependency essentially legitimates women's poverty, whether that poverty is earned through low-paid employment or assigned by subsistence-level benefits'.

The 1980s saw a rise in poverty. In 1979 9.4 per cent of the population of Great Britain lived on below half the average income; by 1988 this had risen to 20 per cent (Becker 1991: 1). Throughout the 1980s a number of Acts (in 1980, 1982, 1986 and 1988) have been passed by Parliament with the aim of reducing public expenditure on benefits. Conservative rhetoric justifying this policy emphasizes the importance of self-reliance. However, this rhetoric in no way challenges the dependency of women. Instead, the effects of government legislation have been to encourage reliance on men rather than reliance on the state. Self-reliance for women would mean access to well-paid jobs and adequate and affordable child care. Instead, there has been a decrease in the financial independence of women (Lister 1990).

The worsening situation of women in poverty can be understood in relation to changes in employment and benefits. A rise in

unemployment has been accompanied by an increase in temporary, seasonal and home working. Women occupy the majority of
these jobs, so even when in work they cannot be sure of an adequate or secure income (Millar 1991: 28–30). Changes in the provision of social security have made the situation worse. The increase
in government expenditure on benefits can be largely accounted
for by an increase in the number of claimants. For the unemployed
and for pensioners there have been decreases in real terms (Millar
1991: 31). Cuts in housing benefit affect people on low incomes.
Child benefit was frozen. Millar estimates that over 80 per cent of
couples and 74 per cent of lone families suffered a loss when
income support replaced supplementary benefit under the provision of the 1986 Social Security Act (Millar 1991: 31).

The income support payable to women not in employment is not
sufficient to keep them out of poverty. For women leaving prison,
with little hope of a job, there is always the temptation to supplement their income by crime. Low-level benefit does not allow the
recipient to save against the unexpected, but recent changes
brought about by the Social Security Act 1986 have abolished
'urgent needs payments'. Instead of non-repayable grants, loans
are now made to those who will have to struggle to repay them,
and may be refused to those who would be unable to repay them.
Once again the most deprived are further disadvantaged by the
legal structures provided for their help.

Some women found that the bureaucratic administration of benefits was slow and complicated, leaving them with insufficient
funds for immediate food and warmth.

> I said 'I haven't got any money'. And the woman's telling me
> 'It's nearly eight o'clock, your kids should be in bed'. I said
> 'Well, they've had nothing to eat. I'll put my kids to bed
> hungry and I'll go to bed, but it doesn't solve anything.'
>
> *Janice*

Similar experiences have been documented elsewhere (Townsend
1989). In some areas private landlords will not accept tenants on
housing benefit because it takes too long to receive it. Although it
should be paid within 14 days it can take up to six months.

Many women found the experience of claiming benefit not only
complicated and protracted but also degrading. One woman,
Tracey, told me that she refused to 'sign on' to claim income
support, and when I asked why, she said:

It's just the way they make me feel when I go there, as if to say
I'm down and out. They are just so rude. Because I've worked
for so long I don't need to be talked to like that, I don't need
anyone to think that I'm begging for money.

Nearly twenty years earlier, Marshall (1972) had found that for
many women the experience of claiming, the treatment which they
received, was more frequently criticized than the level of benefit
they received (Millar 1987). The situation is likely to have worsened since current legislation imposes more stringent tests to as-
certain whether or not claimants are 'voluntarily unemployed' or
'actively seeking work' (Millar 1991: 32).

For many women leaving prison, a primary goal is to regain
charge of their children. Wilkinson (1988) found that mothers
whose children had been taken into care under Section 2 of the
Child Care Act, found that Social Services applied for assumption
of parental rights under Section 3 of the same Act. The mothers
felt disadvantaged in their battle with the local authority both
inside and outside prison. On leaving prison they were usually
required to show that they could provide a home before obtaining
custody of their children. Of course, to be considered 'in priority
need' of housing they had to have their children.

4 Health

Women's poverty is a recognized factor in their poor health. Although women live longer than men, throughout their lives they
suffer more physical and mental ill health (Payne 1991b). Both
outside and inside prisons women are more likely than men to
consult a medical practitioner and to be prescribed medication.
High levels of chronic, if not life-threatening, ill health among
women have been variously attributed to the deprivations, both
material and social, which poor women experience, aggravated by
the stress of trying to care for others, especially children, with few
resources and in unsuitable conditions. As women in poverty, ex-
prisoners are likely to have a history of poor health. This is unlikely to have been alleviated by treatment from the Prison Medical Service (Padel and Stevenson 1988). Back in the community
ex-prisoners suffer the threats to health that other women suffer;
they are also likely to need health care in other areas if they are
successfully to change their lives, for example drug and alcohol
addiction and the removal of tattoos.

Drug and alcohol addiction Official statistics show that women
imprisoned for drug offences constitute the largest single category

of women prisoners – 24.8 per cent in 1989 (Home Office 1990b). While this does not mean that all these women have an addiction, it does indicate a high amount of involvement in drug culture. Furthermore, there will be women imprisoned for offences of theft whose offence was an attempt to fund a habit. A recent inspection by the Probation Service revealed a high proportion of women with drug dependency problems (HM Inspectorate of Probation 1991). And some women will be reluctant to admit to an addiction for fear of having their children put into care. Of the 34 women I interviewed, 12 had, at some time in their lives, been addicted to drugs or alcohol. Such women need help to overcome their addiction if they are to change the lifestyle that previously led to prison. There are some programmes in women's prisons which aim to rehabilitate drug and alcohol abusers, but many women are reluctant to discuss their problems in such an authoritarian context. The prison environment is not one which is conducive to the voluntary self-examination necessary to become aware of the patterns of and the reasons for drug abuse. In some prisons, outside agencies come into the prison to offer their services; in some cases women are given temporary release to attend groups in the community. However, for the majority of addicted women there is a need for help after prison. Again the small numbers mean that the most appropriate help is not available. Many women need women-only groups in which to confront their problems. Such groups are only to be found in the larger cities (Carlen 1990: 78–80). Once again the need for specialist facilities is overridden by the economies of scale.

Tattoos Many young women who experience institutional care or custody also acquire tattoos. These visible signs of disaffection or self-detestation endure and serve as permanent reminders of a former status. They may be removed only by expensive medical treatment. If the woman is on an NHS waiting list the matter is not considered life-threatening and so, in the current climate of cuts in resources, the removal of tattoos is not given priority. One of the women I interviewed had obtained a place at an Oxbridge college. Her arms are covered with amateur tattoos from her early life in care. She had already waited for two years to have these removed and had been told that she would probably have to wait a further two or three years. Meanwhile her sense of difference from other young women at college is aggravated by the knowledge that she actually looks very different. On even the hottest days in summer she continues to wear the long sleeves with which she covers these visible signs of her past. Other women have been driven to desperate measures in similar situations:

> (A) young woman recently removed a Star of David from her forehead with a Stanley knife. The scar was terrible but better than the tattoo, she said, because now she could tell people she had been accidentally burned. She . . . was on the NHS waiting list.
>
> (Tchaikovsky 1991a: 14)

Chris Tchaikovsky argues that, if a prisoner wishes, the Prison Medical Service should arrange for the removal of tattoos by the NHS in an outside hospital. Failing this, anyone who leaves prison so visibly stigmatized needs to have her tattoos removed safely and swiftly:

> Surely this most brutal display of disaffection should, rather than sickening and shaming the bearer, sicken and shame those associated with the incarceration and punishment of children and young adults.
>
> (Tchaikovsky 1991a: 14)

This problem is, of course, made worse by the underfunding of the National Health Service. With scarce resources, priority will be given to those conditions which are immediately life-threatening. The quality of life or the impact of this condition on the woman's future life are not easily measured. The problem is seen as an individual's problem, sometimes as a self-inflicted problem. Unless the structural conditions in which it arose are recognized, it will continue to be seen in this way. For an adequate response to such situations there needs to be a change in government policy on health and welfare provision. There needs to be a move away from the current emphasis on individual responsibility and a recognition that the life opportunities afforded to men and women are a product of their relationships to class, ethnicity and gender – a relationship in which wealth and poverty play a role.

> Poverty means powerlessness – a lack of voice, as well as political, economic and social marginalisation. Poor people are denied access to many of the activities and services which are widely taken for granted. They experience the poverty of restricted opportunities and inhibited life chances for themselves and their children.
>
> (Becker 1991: 2)

Adequate provision in the areas of health and housing, education and social security are necessary for all members of society.

Current policies have created division and difference and then blamed the poor for the place they occupy in the social structure. This can be seen in the structural allocation of resources and in the personal responses encountered by the women I interviewed. Yet without a secure base, a sense of place and purpose, the prospects for change are bleak. Without a secure base within society women ex-prisoners will continue to be marginalized and excluded. Poverty underlies the structural blocks to subjective change. Addressing those blocks is a necessary process in facilitating change. Chapter 5 examines the process of change which is possible once those blocks have been overcome.

Note

1 Women imprisoned for non-payment of fines and deportees receive no discharge grant.

5

MOVING ON

It wasn't loss of liberty that made me think I'm
never going to go and do that again. Trust is the
only thing.

Collette

It's the good feeling of once having loved the idea
of being extraordinary, of being different, of
being outside. I've been quite caught by being
ordinary and inside. For example, you get off the
train in the morning, you go up the stairs with
everybody else slogging in to go to work and
there is a feeling that you are part of everybody
and everything.

Fran

Finding a place in the world, being part of that which one once
rejected, being accepted where one was once rejected – these are
the themes that run through the accounts of the women who feel
that they have changed, or are changing, their lives. These women
have moved, or are moving, from living within the shadow of the
prison house. They have overcome not only the pains of imprisonment but also the patterns that led to imprisonment. To do this it is
necessary to establish new patterns, to make choices and changes,
to develop an autonomous self, and to overcome the structural
blocks to that development.

Imprisonment is characterized by loss of identity, by lack of
place, by denial of personal autonomy. The rigours of the process
of reception into the institution inaugurate a regime of seemingly
arbitrary rules and regulations which, while exaggerating notions
of pathology and difference, deny both individuality and mutuality. They deny any sense of the self, acting alone or with others.

Prison imposes passivity or provokes a counter-productive protest which further estranges the self from effective agency. Most of the women who go into prison experience their sentence as a time in which they are stripped of rights and abilities to act as constructive members of a society, as human beings. For some it is a fracture or break in the process of their lives. For many, however, the prison escalates a process begun outside. The denial of the right to act as agents on their own behalf is not new to them. They are accustomed to acting in response to the expectations of others. Gender socialization patterns encourage women to focus on the needs of others (Gilligan 1982) and to follow the guidance of legitimated (male) authority in meeting these needs (Wilson, 1977; Donzelot, 1979; Thane, 1982). In discussing their early lives, many of the women I interviewed were critical of situations in which their needs had not been recognized, although at the time they had not questioned the situation.

This was apparent in Alice's story with which this book begins. As a child her attempts to improve her life were met with the official response that it was not up to her to pick and choose. Other women remembered a similar failure to give any consideration to their interests apart from a domestic context in which they might be traditionally constructed. Lisa was 16 and had recently left care when she became pregnant and gave birth to her first child.

> I knew I was pregnant, I remember going to the doctors and at the time it was quite a natural process what I went through with the doctor and then going to the hospital, but I look back now and think 'They offered me no other options'. I was 16 and, this really plays on my mind, there was nothing else offered me at all. He didn't ask me about whether I was living at home, whether I got support, nothing. I might've just gone ahead and had the baby anyway – I don't know – but that really plays on my mind that I was just not offered.

From the vantage point of a well-developed sense of personal autonomy Lisa now criticizes the way in which those in authority made assumptions on her behalf, and did not present her with or allow her to make a choice.

Lisa's sense of past helplessness in the face of authority is echoed by others. Linda describes her early life as something that happened to her, rather than something she actually participated in or lived through.

I was born in a tiny village, and I lived with foster parents up until the age of 14, and I saw my mother occasionally, and then at 14 they decided I was beyond their control and I was sent back to my mother who decided I was beyond her control and I was taken to court and sent to approved school. And it went on from there, one thing after the other. You get into that system of being in care, approved school's your first step and then it comes borstal, prison. You just get swept into it. They always give you this thing – 'I'm doing it for your own good'.

In breaking the law women do exercise a choice, and appear to be active agents. But they may not be acting on their own behalf. Alice's experience of becoming involved in crime, and continuing to be involved in crime, to please someone else, is not uncommon. Furthermore, even by conforming to one set of expectations by law-breaking (those of a peer group, boyfriend or family) these women were confounding another set of expectations: first, that women do not act, apparently, on their own behalf; and second, that they do not break the law. Whatever the crime for which they are sentenced, these women were also guilty of breaking a gender stereotype that decrees passivity or properly directed activity for women. From this perspective the regime of the prison may be seen as an attempt to deal with women who act, as much as with women who act criminally. However, in removing a woman from society, in reducing a woman's autonomy, the regime works against her changing the pattern of her life. It leaves her, as Alice found, even more susceptible to old influences when she leaves the prison and needs a home, food and friends. Nevertheless, the majority of the women in this study had stayed out of prison for over two years, and had changed their way of life and their view of life. They seemed unlikely to lose their liberty in the future. How, then, had these women overcome both the established patterns that made them vulnerable to prison, and to the debilitating effects of the prison sentence?

Strategies of change

1 Redirection

The early lives of many women were characterized by lack of control and direction, and prison signalled the loss of the little autonomy they had. Re-establishing themselves within society meant a gaining of a sense of self and self-direction. Discussions of choice and control arose frequently in the interviews as women talked about their decisions to prevent a return to prison, to change their relationship to society, to redirect their lives.

> Once you've gone to prison you've written yourself off, and if you want to write yourself back in you have to go as far in – be as complete in affection as the disaffection was.
>
> *Fran*

However, decisions alone were not sufficient: the process of change was usually a long one, involving other people, further experiences and, not infrequently, experience of failure.

Successful change should be seen as a process – a movement towards autonomy or self-direction, and away from control by other people and events. The women who seem most likely to stay out of prison are those who have been able to take control of their lives and so change direction. In this process they experience themselves as changed in attitude and values. Such change involves perseverance and personal struggle, sometimes with long-term support, sometimes with strategically placed help.

Change may appear to have begun at a moment of decision in the woman's life. Several women identified such moments and related those moments to crises, either within or without the prison. Crisis precipitates decision, renders us vulnerable and opens us up to the possibility of change. However, the exploitation of that possibility will depend upon the situation encountered. New ways of seeing and understanding may be obscured unless they are endorsed by a like-minded group. Many women talked of the need to move away from former companions in crime if they were to change their lives, since former companions will assume an old motivation for a new action, and try to reclaim the women for their way of life. Alice tells how she is still contacted by people who do not believe that her current non-involvement in crime is any more than a temporary strategy to pacify her probation officer. For Alice, and the other women, it was necessary to resist the cynicism of former associates and recognize the limitations of that former way of life. This involves struggle in the process of change. Some women gave graphic accounts of events which had begun the movement of change: moments of decision. However, while talking about their lives they recognized an accumulation of factors which had made them open to such moments. They also acknowledged the subsequent support they had received as they pursued their strategies of change. The decision to change direction takes place within a conducive context, and is dependent upon the continuation of such contexts if it is to be successful.

In the following account Collette describes what she sees as her moment of decision to give up drug use and the people who shared that lifestyle.

I did this prison sentence and got out in February '85, still thinking to myself the first thing I'm going to do is go down the 'dilly with my discharge grant. Five hours I waited to score and I paid about five quid just for a brand new syringe and I couldn't get what I wanted, I had to get amps of Physeptone which initially make you quite sick. So I can remember going down to the toilet and having a fix and thinking, 'What was the point? You have waited for 13 months. You have waited for five hours. You've spent all your money, and all you've done is puke up so far.' I just didn't want to know. And something must have happened positively in my head at that point. I moved out of the environment that I was in. I went and booked into bed and breakfast, which was lonely, but I had dissociated with all the friends I had.

Collette's first step in changing her life was to cut herself off from the friends she had and to face the loneliness that this involved. However, further discussion reveals that before discarding old relationship patterns, Collette has actually experienced a new and more positive way of relating to others.

While I was in prison I had a visitor who was a born again Christian. I'm not a religious person at all, but it was someone that my aunt was in the army with during the war and she had contacted her and said: 'Look Collette is in trouble again. Will you go and see her?' I hadn't really heard anything of the real world, I had been involved with lots of dodgy people for years and years. But this woman Nora came to see me, and she didn't throw religion at me at all. She was just a really really nice person and I had never had that before. I think I felt she had faith in me, and I didn't want to let her down.

Collette also reflects on her relationship with her father; her mother had died when she was a child:

My father, throughout my sentences, had written to me, although I would never let him visit me in prison, that would literally have broken his heart. I think he understood so I was forgiven.

Recognizing that their acts have effects, may harm, or have hurt, others, was for other women also a significant factor in the decision to change their lives:

> I've cocked up other people's lives to an extent that nobody's got the right to do. It's so bad what I've done, I just can't be doing with it any more. It's just taken away so much from my life. It's taken away an incredible amount from other people's lives.
>
> *Susan*

The woman becomes aware of the impact that she has, aware of the consequences, or possible consequences, of her actions.

> My father died and it occurred to me for the first time that he could have died whilst I was in prison and I wouldn't have been there. I had seen prison as an occupational hazard rather than a place that would cut you off from things that matter to you.
>
> *Fran*

Her choice of actions becomes related to her choice of outcomes. Exercising choice and control in relation to the people around her is important in the construction of the woman's self-image and in the pattern of life which she follows.

> Then I also met a new set of friends. I was a bit of a novelty to them at first. They had obviously heard on the grapevine that I had been in prison. But they treated me like a normal person and that had never happened before. Friendships, I had never lived anywhere long enough to have friends.
>
> *Collette*

The difficulty of changing the self without changing the circumstances is clearly shown with drug addiction. Norma has served a number of sentences for offences related to her habit. She expressed a wish to give up heroin but her resolution seemed to crumble as she spoke:

> Once you've been used to a certain way of life it's difficult to break away. When I first came out I went right into it straight away but that was only because I was moving with the same people, but since I've kind of cut them all off I had it occasionally, now and again, every other day in fact – I don't inject I just smoke it.

Addicted to the substance (heroin), and to the same way of life, the companions of this milieu offer no alternative. Norma sees no choice but to try to use less, she has no sense of doing something different. Others speak of the influence of companions in non-drug-using contexts. Cara had come out of prison with her confidence destroyed, to a situation in which she had lost her home and her daughter (who had been made a ward of court), and she could not find work.

> I'd met a few people who – their job is either shoplifting, or heisting or whatever and I came very close to actually doing that as well, being with them, seeing all their clothes. I had nothing. I had no things.
>
> *Cara*

The decision to change, to take control, to redirect one's life is not, in itself, sufficient to accomplish change. For the women I interviewed it was necessary that this decision take place within or lead to a context in which the decision was validated by others. That change is both desirable and possible needs to be recognized, not only by the woman ex-prisoner, but also by those around her.

2 *Recognition*

Like Alice, many of the women had experienced the denial of their needs and wishes both as children and as young adults. The recognition they had received had seen them only as outsiders. They had been defined as problems for which others would find a solution. They had been excluded from participation in decisions relating to their lives. By redirecting their lives, the women were moving away from official control, away from prison and into society. They were taking charge of their lives. But this is difficult to sustain when so many factors combine to frustrate attempts to change. As Chapter 4 shows, many women encounter suspicion from the people they wish to join and an all too ready accommodation from the people they wish to leave behind them. The success of their attempts at redirection depends on the recognition that is received. It is particularly important for the woman to receive this recognition from the groups she wishes to join, and to understand why she has been accepted. In this way she comes to recognize herself as others recognize her.

Work was the forum in which most women experienced themselves as useful and valued. While money is necessary, many of the women wanted more than a paid job: they wanted acceptance and recognition.

> I do think work is crucial, not because of the money, but work because you are just a little cog and the coglessness of so many peripheral people keeps them peripheral.
>
> *Fran*

With the metaphor of the cog in the machine, Fran prioritizes the relationship of interdependence as an important factor in becoming acceptable to and accepting of society. If the woman is to change her life she needs to do more than make a decision, she needs to be in a situation where she can make a choice. Moving away from old haunts and companions may be a necessary step. Equally important is establishing new ones. Work played an important role in the lives of the women who had moved towards autonomy.

Collette found work with a voluntary sector organization and as she became more involved with that, she became further removed from her old life: new values replaced the old ones. Initially she was not sure that she would keep to her resolution not to use drugs; initially the job did not engage her:

> I sat behind a typewriter not doing anything for about six weeks and at that time I thought I was going to go back to drugs. Then I didn't and so six and seven weeks went by, and then instead of buying drugs I wanted to buy clothes or something new.

Collette's relationship to the work was changing. She was given more responsibility, she gained promotion, she experienced job satisfaction:

> I got so involved with my job and my commitment to working with offenders and creating opportunities for them, it substituted for perhaps all the crime and excitement.

While in prison, Rene had decided to change her way of life and to start her own business. Initially change for her meant change for her children:

> When I came out I decided I've got to do something constructive with my life. I can't live like this – doing cheques, that's no good. I had to think about my children.

Using the business skills acquired at a college course, Rene did some market research in her area and drew up a plan to open a children's toy shop. She borrowed money from her father and from the bank, and has been financially successful. However, in describing this success she emphasizes not the profits but the local reaction to her enterprise:

> Everybody's congratulated me. Everybody says 'I hope you're not closing, because it's really nice to have a children's shop in Fulham'. I gradually know what they really want. The school knows about me. You know, everybody talks about me. It was really well needed because when I did my market research, they said that to me.

Recognition is extremely important to the developing sense of self. In Alice's story we saw how important recognition was to her, especially recognition from people untouched by the criminal justice system. The difficulty of this struggle is compounded by class and gender differences for Wanda, who spent her childhood in care and custody and was addicted to heroin for some years. Having spent two years in a drug rehabilitation project, she then trained as an aromatherapist. Using this skill she gives treatments from her home in a council property in Clapham, and at a clinic in Surrey one day a week. At the clinic she is made aware of her difference from the other women, staff and clients, whom she meets there:

> I don't think I'm different from anybody else but I do when I'm down working in Surrey because our lifestyles are different.

Wanda attempts to articulate this difference:

> No one's physical down there, no one touches each other – no black people. One woman asked me 'Are you a lesbian?'

Wanda has moved away from one group of people but has not become part of a new network.

> You find people don't trust you because they've got no one to ask. They think 'Well, where's all your friends?' And I don't introduce no one to nobody.

By failing to introduce recent acquaintances to former acquaintances she is acknowledging a fracture in her life. To introduce new friends to old friends is to acknowledge a continuity in association – to reinforce and reproduce a lifestyle and a sense of self mirrored in those chosen companions. This Wanda cannot do. Like Collette, she does not want to reproduce existing patterns –

she wants change. Unfortunately, such change is dependent upon recognition and this involves acceptance by the group to which she aspires. Without such acceptance Wanda is an outsider. She has no one to ease her passage into the new group. She does not want to reinforce her former identity; she is not recognized as having achieved the identity to which she aspires.

> I look after myself. I think I've educated myself a lot better. I'm much more comfortable, safer, and I do make choices. But I do think something's in the blood. I see it now because I'm with regular people. It's been a bit of a shock really. It's felt really crucial to me because I wanted to fit in with ordinary people but I haven't got the bloody what's-its-name to do it.

Wanda struggles with the fact of her difference, aware of keeping secrets (her prison record, her past addiction, her sexuality) in a context which she does not understand and where she feels she is not understood. The skill in aromatherapy is not enough, she needs a lifestyle and manner acceptable to those who dispense and purchase alternative healing strategies. For Collette and Rene the job was a way of gaining access to the community by gaining acceptance from the community, and ultimately contributing to that community. The initial decision, the early steps, are endorsed by the reactions of others, and they become confirmed in the new orientation.

This process is chronicled by Cara, who came out of prison badly affected by the experience:

> I was always crying, I don't think a day passed when I didn't break down and cry. It took me a long time to think that I was a worthwhile person, that I had anything to offer anybody.

She charts her change from her meeting with a worker from Women In Prison who suggested she visit the Creative And Supportive Trust:

> I think it started when I started doing voluntary work, because that gave me somewhere to direct myself, get involved with, and forget about my problems and concentrate on something else. I used to go to CAST all the time, because I had nothing better to do, and just use their phones to ring up various places, DHSS or whatever.

Gradually Cara became aware of a change. From being helped, she wanted to become an active agent in returning help:

I was just there so much I wanted to get involved in what they were doing. I wanted to be more than just a user. I think that because I showed willing they used to give me things to do.

Cara's willingness evoked a response and she had the pleasure of paid work, which combined her wish to contribute with a wish for the personal autonomy conferred by a regular income. However, money was clearly not the sole motivation, as she continued to work voluntarily when the paid work ceased.

Then they were a member of staff short and so they offered me paid work for a short time, which was brilliant because it seemed years since I had money. If I wanted to go out and buy a jumper or a pair of shoes, I could do it. It felt good. I enjoyed what I was doing, even after the paid work finished I just carried on all the time.

Through working with congenial colleagues on a worthwhile project, Cara gained in self-confidence. She has begun to experience herself as someone who can contribute and whose contribution is valued. She is aware that she is changing, new values are replacing former values. She is moving away from relationships based on hierarchy and towards ones based on equality within networks (Gilligan 1982). A job is valued not for its status in the wider world, but for the opportunity which it offers to contribute to the good of the immediate community, in this case the organization. This is apparent in her response to the offer of the job of office cleaner:

Then they offered me the cleaning job, which is something, before I went to prison, I would never have considered. Cleaning was not my scene. It was something I was not ever going to do. There I was doing the cleaning. It was working that was the biggest leap to get me back together. Eventually I got my house all sorted out. I then got my daughter back.

Recognizing, as others recognize, that she is contributing, Cara gains in confidence and is then able to operate successfully in spheres outside the initially empowering workplace.

Cara sees 'the work' as the major factor in her recovery of her sense of self-worth. Collette has the support of significant individuals but still finds her work important. Rene derives satisfaction from her new-found status within the community. But for Wanda the work experience is less satisfactory. It is not enough to do something that is personally pleasing; job satisfaction and acceptance within the community depend on the response to that work.

For some women the education department of the prison had provided their first experience of recognition. There they had felt acknowledged and affirmed in an environment which otherwise denied their sense of self (see pp. 31–3). This experience led some women to seek to develop their education beyond the prison. Others, too, who had no experience of education in prison, looked to formal education as a route to self-empowerment and the means to change.

> I realized while I was there [Greenham Common] that I had no qualifications apart from two O levels. Everybody there had got degrees. Everybody there was really confident about what they were doing. I didn't have that confidence. I didn't feel I could write and I really wanted to write.
>
> *Nicki*

In the supportive atmosphere of a residential college for women returning to education, Nicki was able to experience an emerging confidence and self-esteem.

> I was getting really good marks and getting quite excited about the fact that I could write essays.

Terri, too, found satisfaction in her experience of adult education at a local college of further education:

> I left school at 15 and I did nothing. It's nice to go because I want to, not because I'm being forced to go. I hated school. This is just totally different. I suppose it's because everyone is on first name terms and I suppose you've got a lot more freedom in what you do. At school you are told you have to do this subject, but at college you go because you are interested in what you're doing.

Personal recognition and personal autonomy are singled out as the factors which make education enjoyable. For many of the women education was also seen as the route to a changed lifestyle, one which would involve recognition and autonomy. Nicki discusses this when, as a college student, she writes of her reunion in prison with someone she knew when she was in care:

> I, as were many girls brought up in care and classed as rebellious, was groomed to expect prison as an almost inevitable consequence of being who I am. When I found myself inside East Sutton Park Prison, scrubbing floors alongside Elaine, who I had met in a remand assessment centre when we were

both 12, I realized what a very good job they'd done of making us accept their vision of what we would become. It also made me realize that I, and every other concerned woman, have the power to change their prophesies for ever.

Nicki, like Alice, looks to education as one way of changing the inexorable cycle of abuse-care-prison and finding a personal empowerment. Like others, they intended to acquire the educational qualifications that would equip them for a position in society which would enable them to overcome a history of poverty and imprisonment. In embarking on an educational programme they were preparing themselves for a new life.

3 *Reciprocal relationships*

The women who changed their lives had usually experienced a change in their relationships, a change in how they related to others. This is apparent in Cara's account of her response to the work and people at CAST (see pp. 88–9). There is a shift away from relating within a hierarchy towards relating within a network based on equality.

Re-establishing broken relationships is a problem facing most women who leave prison. Prison is a place which separates people and severs relationships. For the mothers in the sample the greatest loss endured in prison was the separation from their children and the loss of that period of effective involvement in their children's lives. Coming out of prison, they were confronted with the task of reconstructing a relationship with children who had learned to look elsewhere for nurturing support and love. For many of the women this task was successfully accomplished only after they had begun to grow in confidence and build a new life for themselves. Cara's daughter was 18 months old when the sentence began and she spent a year with her grandmother. It was not until Cara was established in work and had her own house that she was able to have her daughter to live with her:

Eventually I got my daughter back. It took time for her to realize that she was back for good. After a while she started wanting her nan but she's the other way now. Whenever she goes to Nottingham, she cries for me.

Cara went on to describe how her daughter would pine for her, if she was away from her for more than a day. This was something that other mothers experienced and, although concerned at the sense of insecurity that this suggests, they were also gratified at being reinstated as the most important person in the child's life. (During the separation from their mother, only one family of children had been cared for by their father.)

Four of the women had had children after their prison sentence. For these women, children were a further example of their capacity to act as good and useful citizens. Child-rearing was presented as an option which had been chosen, rather than one uncritically accepted as a woman's lot. Thus, Olive decided that rather than pursue her education she would give priority to the early years of her children:

> I got into Middlesex Poly, I was accepted, but I had to postpone it, I got in when I hadn't realized that I was pregnant and I postponed it for a year. Now that's she's small I'd like to give her my full attention. I'll start back when the children are going to nursery. I don't want to leave them to anyone else because I've done a lot of work with Ellen and I just couldn't bear the idea of somebody else undoing all that.

Similarly, Beverley prioritizes her child care abilities and finds these endorsed by another parent, who employs her as a childminder:

> I don't trust people looking after my kids. I think he should be near me more for the first few years of his life. I took in Nando, I've been looking after her since she was a little baby. Her mum trusts me. I know they're not allowed in the kitchen. I can take them to the park and things like that and read them books.

For Beverley the decision to be responsible for her child is also a decision to keep away from activities that previously brought her before the court.

> I'm not really into that kind of thing any more. I said to myself since I've got my baby, no I will not do it.

Traditional gender divisions prioritize the domestic role in women's lives and marginalize all other concerns. Furthermore, this domestic role is constructed in relation to a male provider. None of the women in the sample lived out this role. All of the mothers had some paid employment, and two worked from home (Olive and Beverley). None was financially supported by a man. For the women in the sample successfully changing their lives involved a move away from the traditional gender stereotype and a hierarchical pattern of relationships.

In the opening account, Alice tells how she struggled to be acceptable first to the man who introduced her to criminal activity and then to the man who resented her involvement in crime. She tells us that now her struggle is to be free of such emotional and financial dependence on men. For her this is an acceptable goal to aim for. For others it is something achieved. They reject, not necessarily relationships with men, but relationships which demand dependence. Successful in her professional life, Collette decided that she wanted a similar sense of direction and purpose for her personal life:

> I finished a four-year relationship with a guy because I decided it wasn't going anywhere. I didn't want marriage, I don't want to settle down and he was talking about marriage and babies and I just thought 'No'.

Instead of the traditional agenda of goals in a woman's life, Collette has substituted her own which celebrates her autonomy in her personal as well as her professional life:

> Every month or so I would buy something for the house. I replaced all the secondhand bits I got from auctions. I said to myself 'I have done what I set out. I got the job, I held the job, I have done well for the scheme and now I've got the home,' and I said to myself at that point, 'Nothing is going to threaten this ever again'. In August last year my aunt came over from Australia and wanted to stay. She came to stay with me for two months, so I felt acceptance from her, that I had actually got somewhere, and she was very proud.

Collette does not reject the domestic as a sphere of concern. She enthuses about building up a home. For her it is part of the process of taking charge of her life.

> That was the first time ever that I had had a base of my own, and I just grabbed the chance with both hands and never looked back. I loved being on my own at that time – my own four walls, it was beautiful.

She continues to set herself goals, both professionally and personally, and her sense of achievement is heightened by the fact that she reaches the goals which she sets, and that these goals include not only her own well-being but the well-being of others.

Other women discussed marriage, not as a central goal but as one of a number of options available to them.

He's asked me to marry him. I haven't decided yet. I'm doing an access course, that's to do a degree. But then I don't know what I want to do at the moment, because I really would like to work. If I can work I want to work because I'd love to earn my own money. Michael is good to me and he'd give me whatever I want but I want *my* money. I want to do my own thing.

Bella

At the time of the fieldwork eight of the 34 women told me that they were in a long-term heterosexual relationship, and each of these women described the relationship as one of partnership rather than dependence. Ten of the women told me that they were lesbians and two of these women specifically singled out their partners as a contributing factor in their changed attitude to crime and destructive behaviour. Lisa experienced a period of great depression on leaving prison and looking, in vain, for employment. She acknowledges the encouragement she received from her partner:

I got so despondent and Rebecca's been working for eleven years and she is really together. If she hadn't been there pushing me, pushing me, pushing me, I think I'd have just ended up back where I was.

For other women family or friends provided a supportive network. The crucial factor is an empowering relationship within a network, between equals. In experiencing recognition as an equal the woman is further empowered to act as an equal. The balance of power may shift, the woman may move in and out of power in relation to others; according to the circumstances she may feel more or less in control. Nevertheless, she is developing relationships based on equality where the distortion of hierarchy is removed. She is coming to see herself, and others, as worthy of trust and respect.

For many women this is a new pattern. The subordination of their early years, and of traditional gender roles, had been confirmed by their experience of prison. Denial of the self provokes a need for affirmation but within a hierarchy the self will be affirmed as subordinate; recognition is dependent on deference. For some women losing the deference induced by the prison has been extremely difficult, and has proved to be a block to autonomy and reciprocal relationships. Terri is living in a hostel for ex-prisoners and finds that she relates to the staff in a way which denies her own autonomy:

> We have got staff in the office and I am always going down there and saying 'Is there anything you want me to do?' I think to myself 'Why am I doing this?' I come back from college and go in the office and say 'Look what I've done today'.

However, for another woman the authority pattern shifted within the prison and she was able to begin to relate and work effectively with a prison officer. Lisa had been an extremely uncooperative prisoner who had lost most of her remission, when, in a final attempt to find work for her, she was placed with an officer setting up a pre-release scheme:

> I was making posters, doing a lot of administrative things, finding out who's being released, going and seeing them, saying 'Would you like to come on a course?' It was a kind of two-way thing. She just really treated me as an equal. She'd say to me 'What do you think about this?' I don't know what happened to me. I enjoyed being down there and I enjoyed saying my bit.

For Lisa this began a process of change:

> In all this I started seeing the officers as not just a band of people. I started seeing them as individuals. There's good and there's bad, like there is in Safeways, like there is up the high street. I think that helped me a lot when I started to grasp that. And I think Bea was the main person that helped me do that because she treated me like a kind of an equal really.

The process began in prison when Lisa experienced a different way of relating. When her individuality was recognized, she began to recognize the individuality of others. Recognized as a person with rights and responsibilities, she began to see herself in this way, and to see others, too, as people like herself. The distortion of hierarchy was overcome. After prison, Lisa had further opportunities, in her work and her personal life, to develop relationships based on mutuality. In identifying a prison officer – a woman to whom she might be expected to relate only within a formal hierarchy – as a significant agent of change, Lisa illustrates the potential of the most unpromising of situations.

Unfortunately, such potential is rarely exploited. Both inside and outside the prison, women frequently found that they were patronized and infantalized by official agents of social control. Most of the women were dismissive or resentful of the supervision offered; some found it helpful. Few singled out such an experience as a significant factor in their movement towards autonomy and self-direction. The exceptions illustrate the importance of a move away from a context of hierarchy towards one of mutuality. The probation officer or social worker must be prepared to recognize the woman as she is, and to engage with her rather than attempting to control and direct her. Linda considered her former probation officer to be the major factor in her staying out of prison.

> I actually had someone who would listen to what I said I wanted from my life and not what they wanted or what they thought I should have, which is usually to be off drugs.

From recognizing Linda's needs and wishes, the probation officer then proceeded to help Linda to understand her own potential.

> I decided I was going to have control of my life as much as I could do instead of letting other people have control. I never realized that I could have control, but you can.

Few agents of social control, it seems, recognized the potential of the women who sat before them as ex-prisoners. Such recognition came more readily from those who had shared the experience – other ex-prisoners. Many of the women in the sample spoke warmly of the help they had received from WIP and CAST. Like Alice, Laura and Cara, they experienced acceptance, encouragement and practical help in their efforts to change their lives as women after prison.

This chapter has examined the factors affecting radical change in the women's life. These women had done much more than decide to stay out of prison, they had distanced themselves from former associates, they had taken control of their own lives and had, in many cases, become concerned with the empowering of others. When involved in criminal activity they had been active members of the consumer society, buying and selling, legally and illegally. Paula contrasts her former lifestyle with her current one as a worker with a voluntary sector organization. Previously, she says:

> I used to work in fashion. I wore the best clothes. The money was good, I could travel and live a certain kind of life. I used to have parties, friends round, a lot of food and champagne, a bit of cocaine and a bit of grass to entertain people. I was living a lie. I don't want that kind of life.

Now her values have changed:

I wanted to do something more caring, I prefer to work with prisoners. Over the years I've enjoyed the work so well, and I feel I achieve a lot from it, for myself and for people. Tastes that I used to have I don't have any more because I realize that once you're clothed and you're warm, that's good enough.

Cara, too, describes how her perceptions have changed:

Now, everything is back to normal, although I'm a different person, I'm not the same as I was before. I prefer me now. Before, it's not like I had no worries, I mean everyone has problems, whether they be little or big and you deal with them however you deal with them. But I was very green before. I don't just mean about criminal life but life in general. I didn't see any further than my own little world, a few friends and going out Friday nights, sit gossiping. I just had this very, very small and narrow life. I worked as a receptionist. I wasn't interested in any issues in life. I was just blind really. I was just nothing. Although I enjoyed that little nothing that I was, but now I look back and I don't respect myself for it at all. I feel like I've got a purpose in life.

For Cara this purpose coincides with that of the organization for which she works:

I want to help people who are coming out of prison or are in prison, who are in the same position as I was. It isn't easy. You do need help. That is the most important thing.

These women's vision of the world has changed. They now experience society as structured relationships in which they, with others, play a part. The part they play has changed. No longer do they conform to a gender role which demands deference and dependence, or a criminal role which demands distance and distortion. They now relate as equals, and many endeavour to facilitate such a response in others. Conspicuous consumption, or the desire for conspicuous consumption, has been replaced by conscious contribution. They are concerned to be active participants, aware of the rewards of belonging, of being part of a corporate endeavour. They are aware that their actions can contribute to a common good,

rather than contributing to the sum of human misery.

Fran

These subjective changes take place within a structural context. All the women who had achieved the redirection, recognition and reciprocal relationships which facilitated their autonomy had done so from a basis of secure accommodation and/or empowering educational or work-related experience. In this chapter we have seen how important it was for Collette not only to move away from her old life but to find job satisfaction and personal recognition in her new life. Building a new home becomes for her a physical manifestation of the changes she has accomplished. For Nicki and Terri education is the route to self-confidence and self-direction. For others, like Rene, Cara and Fran, work is a way of making a positive contribution and being recognized for so doing. Without such structural preconditions, the subjective change may begin but it is unlikely to develop. It was the women for whom these conditions had not been met who felt insecure about sustaining their new way of life.

Alice has made a decision to change her life. She has determined on redirection. To do this, she says, she needs to discover what is good in her; she needs to recognize her own worth and to have this confirmed by others. She needs to relate to others in a way which affirms her sense of self and self-worth. Meanwhile the patterns of the past still have a strong hold on Alice. Her fear of rejection and and of a possible loss of control coexist with the decision to change. Alice has a secure home but she is looking for a full-time job, or course of study, which will enable her to become the woman she wants to be. Redirection is dependent upon recognition and reciprocal relationships.

Alice struggles between the past and the future; struggles to be able to pick and choose:

> I've made up my mind that I'm not going to offend any more and that's not prison that made me choose that, it was just realizing that you live a certain life and you're destined to live a certain way. . . . I'm determined to do this voluntary work to find out what's good in me because that's all I want. But its just the pain and everything that I can't control in me and the ghost that haunts me and my fear.
>
> *Alice*

The final chapter will discuss what needs to be provided if Alice, and women like her, are to overcome the experience of prison and succeed in their attempts to change. How might we provide the conditions for an empowering change in subjectivity?

6

LOOKING FORWARD: POLICY IMPLICATIONS

This book is about the enabling conditions conducive to women taking charge of their lives and changing them. Thirty-four women form the focus of the discussion. Each of these women has experienced life in prison and life after prison. The majority of the women have now ordered their lives so as to avoid future imprisonment. The difficulties faced, the factors which inhibit and those which facilitate change, and the processes leading to this achievement have been examined in the preceding chapters. This final chapter will summarize the main arguments of the book and will then present the policy implications of this analysis.

To change their lives the women had to recognize the need for and the possibility of taking control. For many of the women early life had been an experience of denial of their needs and their personal worth. Their lives were over-controlled by others. Eight of the women had experienced institutional care, and a further nine had spent their childhood in homes characterized by violence or indifference. The vicissitudes of institutional care and indifferent homes have been discussed in recent studies (Carlen 1987; 1988). The experiences of the women in this study parallel those observed elsewhere. Other people take charge of the woman's life, categorize her and 'place' her according to professional practices and institutional regimes, rather than the individual woman's requirements. Attempts to assert the self, or her needs, are met with increasingly severe responses aimed at containing behaviour considered unacceptable. Alice, and many of the others, chronicled the frustration of failing to find anyone who would recognize who she was and listen to what she wanted. With increasing force, the woman was given the message that she did not belong. For two of the women the sense of misplacement was made stronger earlier by a growing awareness of their sexual orientation. As adolescent lesbians they felt increasingly marginalized from the culture around them, a culture which celebrated heterosexuality and prioritized heterosexual activity for adolescent girls.

Disempowered and displaced, many of the 34, when young, felt discomforted, dislocated and insecure. These feelings were relieved by the use of drugs, including alcohol, or by the excitement and sense of achievement afforded by crime. Drug use provided a feeling of temporary well-being, while criminal activity produced money, goods and acceptance within a specific social group. For some of the women, drug use became drug addiction and crime became a means of supporting a habit. For others, crime was a response to further marginalization, not the marginalization experienced in childhood but that encountered later in life. Four young black women found their educational and job opportunities limited by racism. Like others living in poverty, they felt they had little to lose and much to gain when the opportunity of criminal activity was presented to them.

For many of the women the response to marginalization was to turn away from conventional society to centre on an already marginalized group, through crime. The response to powerlessness was to turn to narcotics and alcohol to escape from or to dull the pain. Neither response was a solution to the problem. Drug use did not give the women any greater control over their lives and frequently resulted in their greater control by others. For 15 of the women, drug use had resulted in a prison sentence, either for the possession of illicit substances or for activity related to their use. For the others, too, criminal activity had resulted in a greater control by others, a further denial of personal autonomy, and a further exclusion. In responding to a denial of personal autonomy these women had made themselves vulnerable to even greater control.

For the women who made such a decision, determining to stay out of prison meant deciding to take control of their lives and moving away from the control of others. For some of the women it meant a further decision: to challenge their marginalization, to find a place as contributing members of society, and to articulate a criticism of the injustice and hypocrisy which they encountered within that society.

At the time of the interviews, 30 of the women had been out of prison for over two years. Some of the women had reoffended within that time but had received non-custodial sentences, that is to say, they had been perceived by the courts as women for whom a different penalty was appropriate. They had begun a process of change which made them appear as less suited to the exclusion and discipline of the prison regime.

At the time of the interviews all the women were satisfactorily housed; none was homeless. Two, in full-time education, were living in hostel accommodation for students: one was in a project for ex-offenders (the North London Education Project), the other in a university hostel. The majority of the women were in rented accommodation: 15 rented from the local council, nine from housing associations and four from private landlords. Four of the women were buying their homes. All who wished to had regained custody of their children.

Approximately half of the women (16) were in full-time employment and seven of those were working with prisoners and ex-prisoners. Four were continuing their education. Two were working part-time and involved in child care. One was retired. Ten were unemployed. Of these, two were registered disabled, two had a drug addiction, and two intended to continue their education. And then there was Alice, in the process of change, involved in education, voluntary work and psychotherapy.

Most of the women were established in their own homes and had lawful pursuits to occupy their time. They had taken control of their lives and placed themselves within the community. The visible indicators of change were the result of the processes of redirection, recognition and reciprocal relationships through which each woman had achieved autonomy and a developed sense of self. This had developed in a context of support in which decisions to redirect their lives had arisen and in which strategies of change had been possible. Such decisions and strategies had enabled the women to claim the power denied them in their early lives and to begin to work against the impact of imprisonment.

Recognition by others, and the opportunity to relate as people of equal worth, had enabled these women to establish themselves in their own eyes, and in the eyes of others, as contributing and valued members of society. The policy implications of their experiences lie in three areas:

1 Sentencing
  No-one should be sent to prison unless there is no alternative.
  Very few women should be imprisoned.
2 Prison regimes
  For the women who go to prison the regimes should be humane
  and attempt to recognize rather than deny human dignity.
3 Post-prison provision
  Women who leave prison need help in overcoming the structural
  blocks to subjective change. The voluntary sector organizations
  and statutory bodies which seek to provide this help should be
  adequately and securely funded.

1 *Sentencing*

A move away from custody

Sentencing women, already excluded from society, to terms of
imprisonment, pushes them further out of that society, compounds
that exclusion and makes reintegration even more difficult. Few of
the women who go to prison are any danger to the public. The
majority are convicted of non-violent offences: property offences
related to theft, handling stolen goods, fraud and forgery (see
Table 2, p. 155). Of the 34 women I interviewed, only three were
convicted of offences involving violence, and even those three
were not likely to be a danger to the general public, or unamenable
to alternative treatment. In matters of sentencing the first point to
make is that women should not be sent to prison unless the circumstances are truly exceptional. Most commentators agree that the
current use of imprisonment should be restricted: 'There is . . .
a strong case for restricting the use of such a socially damaging
and expensive sanction as custody to only those cases where
the offence is particularly serious or the offender is a danger to
society' (Women's National Commission 1991: 11). The Criminal
Justice Act 1991 clearly aims to reduce the prison population by
so restricting the use of custodial sentences. Section 1 of the Act
states that:

> the court should not pass a custodial sentence on the offender
> unless it is of the opinion –
> a) that the offence . . . was so serious that only such a sen-
>   tence can be justified; or
> b) where the offence is a violent or sexual offence, that only
>   such a sentence would be adequate to protect the public
>   from serious harm . . .

Furthermore, the sentencer must state in open court that a custodial sentence is justified on either of these two grounds. There is room for hope here. Similar measures in respect of juveniles and young offenders brought about a decrease in the number of defendants sent to prison (NACRO 1991b: 1). The 1991 Act directs sentencers to consider the offence for which the defendant appears, rather than the history of previous convictions, unless these throw light on the current offence. Thus it is no longer permitted to give a custodial sentence when someone has continued to offend having experienced non-custodial sentences. However, the history of offending may be examined if the court is trying to decide whether the current offence is, for example, a planned burglary or an opportunist crime. Again, this appears to be a move away from the excessive use of custody.

There is a further provision in the Act which aims to reduce the prison population by reducing the number of fine defaulters. In Section 18 the Act introduces the concept of the unit fine. The 'level' or seriousness of the offence will determine the number of 'units' to be levied in fine. The size of the unit will then be related to the amount of disposable income available to the defendant. This should make fines a fairer response to the defendant's situation. In the experimental areas in which this was tried there were reductions in arrears of payment and in imprisonment for default (NACRO 1991b: 3). However, there remains a problem for those with no disposable income if sentencers are unable or unwilling to consider alternatives.

Both the restrictions on custody and the introduction of unit fines should contribute to the reduction of the number of women imprisoned. However, there are aspects of the legislation which may work against this general trend. These can be seen in the provisions on parole and life sentences. The changes in the parole system are based on the recommendations of the Carlisle Committee. Prisoners serving less than four years will now get an automatic supervised release at the half-way point of their sentence. Discretionary parole remains for those serving more than four years, but they will not be eligible for parole until they have completed half their sentence, rather than the present one-third. On release, anyone serving a sentence of over 12 months will be supervised to the point where three-quarters of the sentence is complete. Anyone convicted of another offence before the end of the sentence will be liable to serve the rest of that sentence as well as any new sentence imposed. Both the Carlisle Committee and the government expressed a wish that these provisions be met by a corresponding shortening of sentences. However, apart from reducing the rarely used maximum of ten years to seven years for theft, and 14 to ten years for non-residential burglary, there is no guarantee in the Act that sentences will be reduced to compensate for the changes in parole.

The provisions on life sentences may also give rise to injustice. During the passage of the Bill attempts were made to make life sentences discretionary rather than mandatory in the case of murder. This would allow a recognition of the very different circumstances of the killing within organized crime and the killing in circumstances of emotional distress. Thus women who kill violent and sadistic partners could have their circumstances reflected in their sentence. The government reversed such amendments. Now a woman serving a mandatory life sentence for a domestic murder after suffering many years of brutality, will not have her case considered for parole, while someone convicted of calculated serial rape, and serving a discretionary sentence, may be so considered (NACRO 1991b: 5–6), although the former is less likely to prove a danger to the public.

Provision in the community

If custodial sentences are to be restricted then other sentences need to be explored. Section 6 of the 1991 Act emphasizes that community sentences must only be given where the offence is serious enough to warrant such a restriction of liberty. This is clearly an attempt to prevent the extension of the carceral zone to include those who would not be in danger of imprisonment. If a community-based sentence is imposed it must be made clear that this is for punitive not pastoral concerns.

The Act allows for the combination of probation and community service orders. Here the aim is to provide counsel and support through the punishment. However, the positive aspects of such a combination could be undermined by imposing too disciplinary a framework on people whose lives are chaotic. The higher the number of targets to meet, the greater the possibility of failing to do so. Women with few resources and many demands to meet may find themselves scheduled for failure.

Women who come before the courts need access to groups which will enable them to discover and develop their own resources without the continued threat of judgement and punishment. For many the women-only groups run by the probation service have proved such a support that they have continued to attend after the completion of the order, and have asked if friends and neighbours may attend (Carlen 1990: 73–92). Such groups cannot provide homes and jobs but they can be a source of self-confidence and self-awareness. Unfortunately the restriction of funds to the probation service, and the small number of women clients, make such groups uneconomical. The same is true of groups in which women together face their drug and alcohol addictions. In a recent analysis of current provision Carlen (1990: 58) concludes that 'the best attempts of existing rehabilitative agencies to keep female ex-prisoners out of trouble and out of prison are routinely subverted by sexist ideologies and government policies which narrow the legitimate options of already marginalized women still further'.

Sentencing council

The 1991 Criminal Justice Act is an attempt to reduce custodial sentences where previous appeals to judges and magistrates have failed. However, there is no guarantee that the intentions behind the Act will be successful unless there is a structure within which sentences can be assessed. Andrew Ashworth (1989) has put forward the idea of a sentencing council or commission composed of specialists in the area of criminal justice who will be able to formulate clear and consistent policies by which sentencers may be guided.

These sentiments have been endorsed by a number of commentators, yet attempts by the Labour opposition to amend the 1991 Act by establishing a sentencing council were resisted by the government. Commenting on the final form of the Act, NACRO (1991b: 4) states:

> If the Act's strategy is to succeed, it must counteract the increase in prison numbers resulting from the parole changes, the danger of the new combined orders 'slipping down the tariff' and the prospect of a large increase in the numbers imprisoned for breach of community penalties . . .
>
> In rejecting the case for a Sentencing Council, the Government has rejected the most appropriate potential mechanism for ensuring that its aims are translated into day to day practice.

Without such guidance punitive, and well-meaning, sentencers are likely to impose sentences which seek better to discipline the offender rather than to respond to the offence. The result of an Act which aims to keep people within the community may well be to push the criminalized even further outside.

Abolition

Women in Prison, the voluntary organization that campaigns on behalf of women prisoners, has done much in the last decade to publicize the conditions in women's prisons and to assist women who suffer there. While seeking to ameliorate the situation of these women currently in prison, WIP (1987: 6) is committed to 'in the long term, the dismantling and total abolition of the present barbaric prison system'.

In 1989 Pat Carlen delivered a lecture to the Prison Reform Trust in which she argued that imprisonment for women should be abolished. Her argument is based on the futility, cost and damage of imprisonment and the apparent reluctance of the courts to respond to pressure or pleas. If prison were unavailable, other methods would have to be used for all but the most serious offences. For these serious offenders a maximum of 100 places would be retained. Carlen argues that such an experiment could begin with women because so few women are found guilty of abnormally serious crimes. The argument is developed in Carlen (1990). Such abolition would prevent not only the inappropriate custodial sentencing of women, but also the use of custody for women who breach community orders or fail to pay fines:

> The majority of the poor . . . have little to lose but their freedom, and it is for this reason that imprisonment must be abolished – and not even used when all else fails. The price we pay for the scandal of poverty in this society is that we render the poor ineligible to pay their penal dues.
>
> (Carlen 1990: 124)

Carlen's proposal is perceptive, practical and purposeful. So far it has fallen on deaf ears, probably because, as she recognizes, 'A hallmark of the carceral society is that its members find it difficult to conceive of a penal system lacking imprisonment as the ultimate backup to every type of penalty' (Carlen 1990: 123–4). Or, as Foucault (1991: 232) says: 'We are all aware of the inconveniences of prison, and that it is dangerous when it is not useless. And yet one cannot "see" how to replace it. It is the detestable solution which one seems unable to do without.' Apparently this blindness persists even when alternatives are presented (Carlen 1990). If, then, appeals to justice, efficiency and cost are disregarded, it is likely that prisons will be used for women in the foreseeable future. Are there ways in which this experience might be less damaging and degrading than it is at present?

2 Prison regimes

As we entered the last decade of the twentieth century, prisons were forced into the arena of public debate. On 1 April 1990 a disturbance began at Strangeways Prison in Manchester. It became the worst riot in the history of prisons in the United Kingdom and lasted for 25 days (Woolf and Tumim 1991: 3). It was followed by a series of riots by prisoners in other prisons throughout the country. There were, however, no similar riots in any of the women's prisons. The only involvement of women arose when the governor of Pucklechurch requested that the women on remand at his prison be moved. He could not guarantee their safety as the men at Pucklechurch rioted (Tchaikovsky 1991b: 12).

As a result of the riots of April 1990 an investigation was undertaken by Lord Justice Woolf and Judge Stephen Tumim. The report which followed, in February 1991, the Woolf Report, has been recognized as one of the most important investigations of Britain's prison system (Sampson 1991: 1). It is particularly noteworthy as an official document which gives a voice not only to employees, from governors to the most junior officers, but also to the prisoners, that is, to male prisoners. The Woolf team visited Holloway and spoke to senior members of staff but not to the women prisoners (Liebling 1991: 4). The final report does not address issues which relate solely to women as women were not involved in the rioting. However, there are recommendations in the report which, if implemented, would affect women, possibly adversely. The wish to accommodate prisoners near to their homes, and thus make it easier to maintain ties with families and friends, has resulted in the suggestion that community prisons be established. These would each be divided into different units to cater for different types of prisoners, for example, remand prisoners, young offenders, sex offenders and women. Thus the issue of mixed prisons has again arisen as a solution not to women's problems but to the needs of a

system designed primarily for men. The advantage for women of
proximity to families and friends must, in such circumstances, be
considered in relation to the realities of life where women and men
share the same resources. Chris Tchaikovsky (1991b: 12) argues
that women would suffer wherever resources were limited.

> Experience has shown this to be the case and with far more
> sinister implications for women than being last in the queue for
> the gym, cold food or a hands-on session in computer skills.
> It emerged at the inquest on one of the nastiest deaths of a
> woman in custody, that the resuscitation equipment took
> almost a quarter of an hour to be brought to the women's wing
> from the men's hospital. At Durham H Wing, it was not a
> question of cold, but contaminated food. The contempt from a
> number of male prisoners for their female counterparts was
> revealed by the spitting on, and urinating in, the women's food
> and drink. So, it really isn't a question of sharing resources or of
> women not getting their fair share – more a total lack of under-
> standing of the base reality of day-to-day prison life.

In the same article, Tchaikovsky refers her readers to research
revealing a high proportion, among women prisoners, of victims of
abuse by men (Posen 1988). For such women the proximity of men
increases the pain of imprisonment. While Woolf and Tumin may
recommend that women be held 'in a wholly secure and separate
block', the experience at Pucklechurch suggests that this is not
feasible. Even the extremes of technology employed at Durham,
with all the ensuing disorientation, do not ensure that women are
safe from abuse by men (Padel and Stevenson 1988: 108–24).

The Woolf Report was welcomed by the government and followed, in September 1991, by a White Paper, *Custody, Care and
Justice: The Way Ahead for the Prison Service in England and
Wales* (Home Office 1991). In the White Paper the government
accepts the principal proposals of the Woolf Report and sets out a
programme for change. Once again, women prisoners are an ad-
junct to the system rather than a client group in their own right.
The White Paper states that:

> it is preferable that women prisoners should be located as
> near to their homes as possible: where location of female
> establishments is particularly poor, it may be necessary, after
> full consultation both within and outside the Prison Service, to
> consider the possibility of accommodating women prisoners
> in establishments shared with male prisoners, provided the

accommodation is separate, fully secure and of an adequate size, and that the women will have satisfactory facilities and regime activities.

(Home Office 1991: 5.14)

Of course the White Paper takes up other recommendations from the Woolf Report, and these should improve the situation of all prisoners, men and women. These include the provision of sentence plans so that prisoners are aware of how their time is to be usefully deployed (7.18); the provision of explanations for decisions relating to prisoners (7.20); the improvement of physical conditions (6.1–22); better facilities for education and employment (7.21–6); and increased use of home leave and extended and informal visits (7.36, 37). Furthermore, the White Paper promised the provision of guidance specifically for women's prisons (7.15). The guidance, *Regimes for Women* (HM Prison Service 1992), was issued in February 1992.

The purpose of the guidance, is to identify good practice in establishments for women, in order that such practice might be emulated elsewhere. 'Good practice' is defined as that which contributes to the provision of 'appropriate and humane regimes' (HM Prison Service 1992: para. 1). The guidance emphasizes that women prisoners must be treated with respect and given a voice in the day-to-day organization of the institution (paras 4 and 9). The use of consultative committees of prisoners is commended (paras 10 and 11). The overuse of disciplinary charges is criticized (paras 107, 108 and 110).

Unfortunately, the guidance also endorses the current practice of insisting on closed conditions for foreign nationals facing deportation at the end of their sentences (para. 11b). This practice is justified by a claim that such prisoners are likely to abscond from an open prison, since some have already done so. Such a blanket decree does not allow prison staff to assess the likelihood of any individual woman's absconding. The result is that long sentences are being served under the most restricted regimes. Mothers suffer a further penalty since they may keep their babies for a shorter time. The mother and baby units of closed prisons usually allow the children to remain for only nine months, and, even if this period is extended, the conditions are most unsuitable for young children. So, because they are not British, these women are sentenced to greater exclusion, and further removed from non-prison life.

However, there are at present in women's prisons a number of schemes which challenge the traditional divisions between prison and non-prison life, and these the guidance commends. These schemes operate in the following areas:

1 visits
2 education and unemployment
3 drug and alcohol rehabilitation programmes.

1 *Visits*

Visits are important to all prisoners since they afford some contact with the outside world and a chance to recapture, albeit briefly, a non-prisoner identity. For the mothers of young children they are the only means of communication. However, the timing and place of traditional prison visits often creates awkwardness between adults and even more difficulties when trying to relate to a child. Experiments to reduce such difficulties are vital. In Askham Grange women are allowed to regulate their own visiting hours within wide boundaries. In Holloway the visitors' room has been decorated by the art teacher so that panels around the walls present a number of stimulating images in the styles of different artists. However, the most acclaimed of the innovations in this area is the extended visit scheme at Holloway, whereby children are able to spend a full day with their mothers. On two Sundays a month children are allowed to visit from 9.30 a.m. to 3.00 p.m. On these Sundays thirty women are able to spend time with their children in a number of venues which are adapted to provide activities and spaces to promote positive interaction. Priority is given to those who have not experienced such a visit. Prison staff and volunteers from Save the Children are present to offer help. A Mothers' Committee consisting primarily of women prisoners, but with a representative from Save the Children and two members of staff, organizes the days and plans for the future.

The scheme is to be formally evaluated by the prison Psychology Department but has already been enthusiastically welcomed by many of the prisoners as an opportunity to relate to their children. Styal has now launched a similar scheme.

Extended visits are undoubtedly an improvement on the shorter visits in a formal setting. However, problems of space mean that no child may visit his or her mother more than once a month, and pressure of numbers might make visits even less frequent. There is a danger that the publicity surrounding such visits may reduce a sentencer's concern at imprisoning a mother. There are also implications for the greater control of mothers who may fear the loss of such a visit. Instead of focusing on bringing children into prisons, we need to look at ways of taking mothers out of prison. Home leave could be used imaginatively to enable mothers to spend time with their children in a familiar environment. This would not only promote good mother–child relations, but would also lessen the institutionalization of the mother. For those imprisoned at some distance from their families, the ease and expense of travel for one adult would be much less than for an adult carer and a number of children. Moving out of prison is the surest way to lessen the impact of incarceration. This has been most successfully done in relation to education and employment.

2 *Education and employment*

Women's prisons aim to provide education and training opportunities as well as employment experience. However, the small numbers, particularly of long-term prisoners, make it impractical to offer a wide range of subjects and activities. Some prisons have turned to the community to meet the need. Drake Hall is one of a number of establishments which make use of local colleges to enable women to follow courses outside the prison. Holloway, too, has a number of women attending colleges outside the prison.

Holloway also has up to 12 women a day attending the NACRO Job Club outside the prison. Here women gain confidence and acquire job hunting skills. They may go for an interview and accept a job which they can begin up to three months before their release date. Holloway now has a number of women in paid and voluntary employment who are away from the prison all day but return in the evening after work.

Such schemes do much to reintegrate the women into society, but, inevitably, they raise questions about the appropriateness of holding such women in prison. Perhaps some would wish to argue that the women's suffering, and the public expense, are justified in terms of punishment for crimes committed. Certainly these women are no danger to the public. It could be argued that a woman who may be trusted to undertake employment and return each evening is thus demonstrating that she ought not to be in prison at all.

3 *Drug and alcohol rehabilitation*

A high proportion of women serve prison sentences for drug-related offences. A recent estimate put the number in Holloway at 40 per cent (Matthews 1991: 12). In *Regimes for Women*, the Home Office reiterates that all prisons should have facilities for 'drug misusers'. Holloway is singled out for particular praise in this matter: 'Exemplary arrangements for detoxification, together with officer-led drugs courses have been introduced at Holloway' (HM Prison Service 1992: para. 81). This is a reference to the 'Hope, Health and Happiness' project aimed at alcohol and drug users. The project offered a six-week programme providing information, counselling and awareness of relevant outside agencies. A new programme is now being developed which will consider the possibility of a residential drug rehabilitation unit within the prison. Once again this will be staffed by committed officers with some training, and will also involve professionals in this area and ex-users.

Given the detrimental effect that drugs and alcohol have had on the lives of many women prisoners, there can be no doubt about the need for specialized programmes. The question which arises concerns the suitability of the prison as a place for such programmes and of disciplinary staff as the facilitators of such programmes. If addiction lies behind the crime then it is debatable whether punishment by imprisonment is an appropriate response. If prisons are places where rehabilitation is seen to take place, there is an added incentive for the punitively minded sentencer to advocate custody.

Regimes for Women applauds both the officer-led programmes at Holloway and the use of outside agencies which can provide help within the prison but also introduce the women to facilities outside the prison (paras 18, 81). By making women aware of the agencies available, and allowing them out of the prison to use such agencies, the prison becomes less estranged from the outside world. By using facilities within the community the prisoner is beginning a rehabilitation process within the community, where rehabilitation and reintegration must take place if they are to be successful.

If the aims of the 1991 Criminal Justice Act are realized, fewer men and far fewer women will go to prison. If this happens then the provision of a range of programmes within the prison will be even less feasible. To meet the different needs of different women, the prison will have to look to those agencies which seek to meet the need outside the prison. Attempts to duplicate resources will not only prove costly but also provide a dangerous justification for those who wish to argue for the continued imprisonment of women who need help not punishment.

What the prison can and should provide is a regime which does as little damage as possible to the women under its jurisdiction. As the current guidance advocates, this will involve a reception process which is sensitive to the bewilderment and distress of women entering prison. It will involve an induction process by which women are familiarized with the routines and the necessary rules of the institution. There will be a sentence plan, regularly reviewed, so that women are aware of the reasons for the activities in which they are engaged. Prior to release, prisoners will undergo a pre-release programme to prepare them for life outside.

The identity of 'prisoner' is fostered in the environment of the total institution, the all-embracing prison. If the hold is weakened, if the totality of the institution is fractured, then the identity will be less confirmed. It is only to the extent that women have been completely removed from society that they require projects and programmes to return them to that society. Unfortunately, there is today still much need of such post-prison provision.

3 *Post-prison provision*

Many of the women who go to prison have few ties to the community. Many have experienced institutional care and have no stable family base. Many are homeless or lacking secure accommodation (Wilkinson 1988: 160; Carlen 1990: 40). Many are unemployed. Furthermore, imprisonment is likely to weaken or destroy the ties that do exist. It removes the woman from society not only for the present but also for the future. The totality of the prison regime forces the woman to acknowledge and adapt to that regime, thus making her less fitted than before for life away from the institution (see Chapters 2 and 3). Even the best constructed of pre-release courses cannot counteract the impact of months or years in a situation of powerlessness and exclusion. Women who leave prison need help in returning to society, in combating the effects of imprisonment. They need homes and jobs, and emotional support. They need what all women need, but unless they can move back into society those needs will not be met (see Chapters 4 and 5).

The woman who leaves prison faces the choice of surveillance or secrecy. If she admits to her past she is frequently subject to further control and exclusion; if she does not, she lives with a guilty secret and the constant fear of exposure. Post-prison provision needs to be such that the woman feels accepted and encouraged to become responsible for her own actions, and for her own life. To move into a new life many women need a transitional period during which they re-evaluate and move away from the attitudes and values which characterized their lives before and during prison.

For women disempowered by the experience of prison and lacking a secure base in the community, there is a need for organizations and individuals able to co-ordinate the women's needs and match them to the available resources. For some women this will be done by a good probation officer. Others may need to seek help from the voluntary sector. There are eight relevant organizations for women who want the support and reassurance of a woman's organization which can recognize and respond to their needs as ex-prisoners: Women In Prison (WIP), Creative And Supportive Trust (CAST), Women Prisoners' Resource Centre (WPRC), Black Female Prisoners' Scheme (BPFS), Female Prisoners' Welfare Project (FPWP), African Prisoners' Scheme (APS) and Akina Mama Wa Afrika. For women leaving special hospitals and prison psychiatric units there is Women in Special Hospitals (WISH). All eight are voluntary sector organizations which aim to help ex-prisoners in their return to the community. They enable women to confront the structural blocks to change by providing help and advice on housing, education and training, jobs, dealings with the DSS and other areas in which women need support. In this way these organizations provide a space within which women can develop a new sense of self and from which women can begin to take control of their lives.

WIP deals mainly with women in prison, but this frequently involves arranging accommodation for women before, or shortly after, they leave prison. The welfare worker at WIP is familiar with the range of housing facilities which are available for women and also has contacts within many of the local authority housing departments. WIP workers also give advice on other matters, particularly in relation to education and welfare. This aspect of the work of WIP arises as a consequence of the organization's concern for women prisoners, a concern which does not cease once the women walk out of the prison gates. However, WIP does not claim to provide a post-prison provision programme.

WISH extends the service provided by WIP and addresses the needs of women in special hospitals. Like WIP, WISH is involved in finding accommodation, training and education placements and offering other forms of support to women as they return to society.

While many black women use the other projects, BFPS caters for black women who want the support of a project run by black women and focusing on their needs. Welfare workers from BFPS visit all the women's prisons and offer a counselling and advice service for those who have left prison. APS and Akina Mama Wa Afrika offer a similar service to African women.

WPRC is part of NACRO. The aim of the organization is to assist women who are trying to return to the community after prison. WPRC workers visit prisons and provide advice and information on housing, health, education, employment, welfare and legal matters. There is also a London base which women may ring for advice and use as an informal drop-in centre. WPRC is particularly concerned to encourage other agencies to make their resources accessible to women ex-prisoners.

FPWP is concerned with foreign nationals who serve sentences in British prisons. These sentences are usually long ones, for the importation of drugs. They are imposed without the mitigation that might be offered by a social enquiry report, and the chances of parole are reduced if there is no way of obtaining a home circumstances report. During their sentences many women suffer acute anxiety about their children, now abandoned to poverty in countries with little welfare provision. Furthermore, on their return home, as deportees and ex-prisoners, these women have no organizations to offer support, advice or help. Women from Nigeria face further difficulties since, under Decree 33, the Nigerian government is threatening to impose a further five-year sentence on those who have been imprisoned for drug related offences in the UK.

FPWP has set up a project in Lagos, Nigeria – the Hibiscus Project – which employs workers who are able to produce social enquiry reports and home circumstances reports for women from Lagos. Such reports have helped to reduce sentences and increase the likelihood of parole. The project workers are also able to locate and help many of the children of prisoners and on the women's release they provide support and guidance. FPWP hopes to extend the facility to the West Indies and South America by setting up projects in Jamaica and Colombia.

CAST workers visit prisons but the main part of CAST's work is post-prison provision for women. Like WIP and FPWP, CAST was founded by ex-prisoners and employs a number of ex-prisoners. It aims:

to provide a bedrock from where women ex-prisoners can start to rebuild their lives and can be provided with the skills which they believe will be necessary for this purpose . . . a place where they could be open about their prison experience, gain support and be accepted.

(CAST 1991: 2)

CAST employs a welfare worker to give advice. There are weekly drop-in sessions and there is the opportunity to make an appointment with the welfare worker. However, the main focus of CAST's work is on the provision of education and training. The courses are accredited and aim to develop skills and confidence and so prepare women for further education and employment. In 1991 courses were offered in: art and design, confidence and communication, English, information technology, photography, and self-defence. There is a constant monitoring and evaluation of the programme so that the organization can respond to the needs of the women clients.

Between April 1991 and November 1991, 177 women turned to CAST for help in the following areas: housing, 76 (43 per cent); child care, 16 (9 per cent); education and training, 98 (55 per cent); health matters, 16 (9 per cent); legal issues, 11 (6 per cent); and general support 21 (12 per cent) (CAST 1991). Housing, education and training, then, are areas of importance to women contacting CAST. Housing is a priority for many of the women who contact the other groups, but they, too, receive requests for help on matters relating to education, training and welfare. Recognizing common interests and a common constituency, the women's organizations have representatives on the Women Prisoners' Action Committee, which meets to identify needs and to ensure an equitable spread of scarce resources. Women leaving prison need specialist help in:

1 housing
2 education, training and employment
3 welfare and general support.

1 *Housing*

While many women are homeless before going to prison, others become homeless through being in prison. Although housing benefit may be used to pay for up to 12 months' rent, many women are unaware of this, unaware of how to claim, or too bewildered by the process and their own situation to do so. Others may lose their homes through vandalism or squatting (Carlen 1990: 41).

Women leaving prison face accommodation problems both as women and as ex-prisoners. As women they are a minority of ex-prisoners. As prisoners they may be unable to give a specific date of release. Without a specific date a hostel may be unwilling to give the guaranteed place which the woman needs to obtain parole. Those agencies which understand and cater for the situation of ex-prisoners may find that there is pressure to take the many more men requiring beds. As a result women are greatly outnumbered in the hostel or unaccommodated. Many women express a wish to live away from men when they first leave prison (Carlen 1990: 45). This may be the result of a history of abuse, from a wish to adjust slowly to a mixed-sex environment, or from personal preference.

What these women need are spaces where they feel secure during this time of readjustment. For some, security will mean a structured environment with supportive staff on site. In such cases rules and regulations may be part of that useful support. For others such a regime is too reminiscent of the prison and they seek a freer environment. Proper provision for women ex-prisoners cannot be a uniform provision. Apart from variations in the degree of structure and formal support that is needed, women also have other characteristics which should be recognized in their accommodation. They may have dependent children. They may want to live with other lesbians or black women. They may have a history of violence or arson. They may need help with drug or alcohol problems. Or they may require none of these but a temporary base from which to move into a permanent affordable home.

Most prisoners are from the already disadvantaged sectors of society, and share the problems of other women in poverty. Like them, they will be particularly affected by the government's housing policy during the last decade. The sale of council houses and the consequent loss of low-cost rented accommodation has had its impact on this group. Such women are also likely to be disadvantaged by statutory provision and local policy in the assignment of available accommodation. The 1985 Housing Act obliges local authorities to offer permanent accommodation only to those 'in priority need'. This usually means those with dependent children, those who are pregnant or those defined as 'vulnerable'. Those whose children are in care will need accommodation before they can take them back, but such accommodation may not be granted until the mother is, once again, responsible for her children.

Even if a woman is defined as being 'in priority need' she will need to prove a 'local connection' to the authority with whom she seeks housing. This will pose a problem for those who have lived an itinerant life prior to prison. Furthermore, some women may wish to leave old haunts and be housed in new areas in order to avoid former criminal contacts. Housing such women in their former localities may well prove counter-productive.

A woman also needs to prove that she has at no time made herself intentionally homeless. Yet if she has at any time given up a home or lost one through eviction, a council may decide that she has made herself intentionally homeless. Such a decision ignores the structural realities of life for many women who go to prison. For them violent partners, poverty or disorganization may have resulted in the loss of a home. Unaware of these dynamics, others may consider that the woman has made herself intentionally homeless.

Women who are without a home or children are penalized by current policy and practice concerning the allocation of housing. Women who are poor are among those most affected by the un-availability of housing. What is needed is government investment in low-cost housing to meet the needs of the currently homeless and those living in bed and breakfast accommodation. This is needed by all women living in situations of poverty. For those with specific problems, particularly for ex-prisoners, there is a need for a range of hostel provision designed to meet differing needs. Such provision for a relatively small group of women will be expensive, but the cost should be seen in relation to the greater cost of imprisonment. Without this opportunity to establish a secure base, their own place in society, women are subject to former patterns and processes. They are denied the opportunity to redirect their lives.

2 Education, training and employment

As we saw in Chapter 4, women leaving prison lack confidence and feel particularly vulnerable in public settings. While the usual provision for education and training gives opportunities for acquiring skills and so building confidence, traditional classrooms may prove too daunting a prospect to be useful. CAST recognizes this and provides creative vocational and self-development courses on a modular basis. These short courses give women the opportunity of acquiring skills in a supportive atmosphere (see Meg's discussion of CAST in Chapter 4). Women are then encouraged to move on to other courses in local colleges. CAST is based in Camden, London. London has two other projects which provide educational advice and run courses specifically for ex-prisoners. Both the North London Education Project and Southwark Offenders Learning Opportunities provide advice on courses and grants. NLEP does more. It provides accommodation, with, if needed, separate accommodation for women, and staff to support ex-offenders in full-time education. Throughout the rest of the UK there are a number of education and training projects for ex-prisoners run by NACRO. None of the projects is for women only (Carlen 1990: 92).

Both CAST and NLEP offer an exceptional and badly needed service for women ex-prisoners returning to education. CAST does this by gearing courses to the needs of women in this situation. NLEP provides accommodation and support for women in adult education within the local community. In both contexts women have the space in which to acknowledge their past and the impact that this has on their present. They are then better able to move on to a new way of life unencumbered, at least in this context, by secrecy or surveillance, the fear of discovery or the experience of further control. However, as Pat Carlen (1990: 92–6) has documented in detail, such projects are at risk from changes in direct funding and as a consequence of other changes in public spending on education and social services. Such projects need to be secure in their resources and should be extended throughout the country, or at least to other major cities. As many of the women I interviewed testified, it is in ex-prisoner groups, and usually in all-women ex-prisoner groups, that they began to gain the confidence to move back into society. The recognition they received, and the changes they recognized in themselves, were a necessary part of this process.

Employment was another way in which women experienced themselves as useful and valued by others. Sometimes this involved working with other women in similar situations. Sometimes it involved drawing on the confidence and skills gained in education and moving into new and challenging situations. However, the workplace is a site which immediately poses the problems of secrecy or surveillance. To tell of her prison past often means that a woman will not be employed; to keep her past secret means that she lives in fear of discovery. In interview many of the women expressed the view that a change of attitude by employers would be the single most useful step in the reintegration of ex-prisoners into the community. There are organizations which are concerned with finding employment for people with criminal records, the two biggest being NACRO and Apex.

Currently, Government policy is threatening the very existence of Apex and has resulted in a cut of over 50 per cent in NACRO's provision.

> Those cuts which NACRO suffered in common with other voluntary organizations providing Youth Training and Employment Training for disadvantaged people, resulted from an overall reduction in the Government's training budget and from the introduction of Training and Enterprise Councils (TECs) – whose priorities generally lie with those who can get jobs and qualifications quickly.
>
> (NACRO 1991a: 11)

Unfortunately, there is little recognition of the specific employment needs of women, or even that employment is a major issue for women (Carlen 1990: 97). Issues such as housing, children and personal relationships are more associated with women. The evidence of the 34 women that I interviewed suggests, however, that employment, training and education are important to women. Of the ten who were not so occupied, two were involved in child care, two were registered disabled, and two were drug addicts. Thus of the 34 women, only four who were available for work were not employed, and two of these intended to continue their education. For women intending to change their lives and stay out of prison, education and employment have an important role to play. Women leaving prison need the opportunities to pursue these goals in open and supportive settings. Again, the cost of properly resourcing the organizations which respond to the needs of women ex-prisoners should be set against the greater cost of future imprisonment.

3 Welfare and general support

There are, of course, other areas in which women need help if they are to accomplish a successful transition from prison back to society. There are the more widely experienced problems such as claiming full benefit entitlement or regaining the custody of children in care. There are problems specific to individual women. One of the women I interviewed was anxious about the length of time it was taking for her child to be adopted by his foster parents. Another woman was having problems finding a GP willing to accept her; this she attributed to a chronic condition made worse by her experience of prison. Such matters are currently dealt with by probation officers as well as by the voluntary sector organizations. At present, women who serve short sentences are not subject to supervision but the numbers to be supervised in the community will increase under the provisions of the 1991 Criminal Justice Act. There are individual probation officers who are informed on and sympathetic to the problems of women ex-prisoners. There are also probation services which prioritize such issues. However, the services are primarily geared to the needs of men who constitute the majority of clients. Some female clients have expressed a dissatisfaction, particularly with male officers. Some female probation officers have reported problems with male colleagues who oppose attempts to prioritize the needs of female clients, for example in the running of all-women groups (Carlen 1990: 71–92). There is a strong argument for women to have the option of a female officer. A recent report from NACRO has argued that the 1991 Criminal Justice Act could be effective in promoting the widespread adoption of the best of probation practice:

> Within the context of implementing the Criminal Justice Act, the Government intends to ensure that all services follow national policies and meet national standards. These should include strategies for the work of the service in relation to the resettlement of women. It could include ensuring that women have the option of a female probation officer, and access to women's groups. It would ensure that the needs of women who have been victims of violence or abuse from men are taken into account in service provision.
>
> (NACRO 1992: 5.16)

Whatever is effected through the statutory bodies, there will still be a need for the voluntary sector organizations which are primarily concerned with women prisoners, both during their sentences and on release. In changing times they focus on the needs of these women, seek to meet them with available resources and campaign for provision in areas unaddressed by current provision. Any serious attempt to provide for the reintegration of women prisoners should begin with the adequate funding of the eight organizations, mentioned above, which have prioritized their needs.

These organizations aim to give women access to the contexts within which change is facilitated. For too long women have been penalized because of their small numbers within the criminal justice system. Provision, both within and beyond prison, has been aimed at the majority male population. Women have their own needs as women and as women prisoners and these must be acknowledged if they are to be given the space from which to move back into a society which has marginalized and excluded them. We must provide the structural preconditions of place and purpose – of home, education and employment – if women are to embark upon the redirection, recognition and reciprocal relationships by which they reorder their lives.

APPENDIX 1
DOING THE RESEARCH

1 *Posing the problem*

The last decade has seen the publication of a small but growing body of work on women's prisons and women prisoners in the United Kingdom (Carlen 1983; Carlen *et al.* 1985; Peckham 1985; Dobash *et al.* 1986; Mandaraka-Sheppard 1986; Women's Equality Group/London Strategic Policy Unit 1987; Padel and Stevenson 1988). It has also seen the founding of Women In Prison, the voluntary sector organization committed to publicizing the conditions within women's prisons (Carlen and Tchaikovsky 1985). For the interested public there are now a number of sources of information and analysis of the situation of women prisoners. From the official statistics we learn that women form a small proportion of the prison population. In 1989 they constituted 3.6 per cent of the prison population in England and Wales (Women's National Commission 1991: 2). Few of these women are held for violent or sexual offences; in 1989 these offences accounted for 7 per cent of women sentenced (see Table 2, p. 155). The cost of holding a woman in custody was, on average, £399 per week for 1988–9, while sentences served within the community, such as community service, probation and supervision orders, cost less than £20 per week (Women's National Commission 1991: 3). There are, however, other costs incurred by imprisoning these women. Separation from families, particularly from young children, causes pain to the women and to the family members. An examination of the characteristics of the female prison population reveals that these women are often among the most damaged and disadvantaged in society (Carlen 1988). Many have few ties to the community. Imprisonment strains and frequently severs the ties that do exist. Through imprisonment women may lose, if they have them, homes and jobs, friends and family. The small number of women prisoners means a small number of women's prisons scattered throughout the country (see Figure 1 on p. 158). Women are likely to be imprisoned at some distance from their homes and this makes visits, particularly with young children, awkward and expensive.

The experience of imprisonment is not one to equip a woman to cope more effectively with life:

'Analysis of the regimes in the women's prisons leads us to conclude that the motto of those running them could well be summed up by the slogan "Discipline, Infantilize, Feminize, Medicalize and Domesticate" ' (Carlen and Tchaikovsky 1985: 182). So what happens to women who go through the experience of prison? The rate of recidivism is lower for women than for men. Of prisoners released in 1986, 50 per cent of men, but only 34 per cent of women, had been reconvicted within two years (NACRO National Policy Committee on Resettlement 1992). Two-thirds of women, then, manage to stay out of prison. To what extent does this involve making significant changes in their lives? How are such changes accomplished? What are the obstacles to such changes? These were the questions that prompted the present research. To pursue them further I needed access to the women for whom this process was a fact of life. I needed to talk to, or rather listen to, women who had experienced prison, and were prepared to reflect on their experiences.

2 Locating the sample

At this stage I was fortunate in receiving encouragement and help from Women In Prison, particularly from the director. She contacted a number of women on my behalf and asked if they would be willing to be interviewed. All agreed – I do not know whether this was a result of the director's skill in choosing possible subjects or her persuasive powers when explaining the project. I then

telephoned each woman and arranged to meet her. In most cases
the interviews took place in the woman's home, usually within the
following two days. Five women were interviewed at their place of
work in a voluntary sector organization. Three women were interviewed at the offices of WIP. One woman was interviewed at my
office in Central London. One interview was conducted in a pub
but later followed up at the offices of WIP.

When I first described the project to the director of WIP I said
that I was interested in the prison experiences and post-prison
experiences of all women and I asked that none should be excluded on the grounds of the untypicality of her crime or her
circumstances. There was a deliberate decision at this stage to
include four women imprisoned for action at Greenham Common.
Three of these women (Barbara, Judith and Martha) felt that their
experiences were too unlike those of other prisoners to be useful.
However, there was in these differences the source of useful comment on the more usual experiences of other women prisoners.
Throughout their sentences, members of the Greenham Common
peace camp received letters and flowers from those outside. This
lessened their sense of separation from the wider world. Indeed,
these women were not excluded by their community and were
continually reminded, through the letters and flowers, of their inclusion, by their actions, in the aims and objectives of camp members. However, even though prison was a rational choice, made to
further the cause, and even with the extraordinary level of support
that these women received, it was not enough to counteract the
impact of prison on their sense of self. With less support and
longer sentences other women are likely to be even more susceptible to the influences of the prison regime.

Some of the women whom I met through WIP then referred me
to other ex-prisoners and so my sample grew. The total number
interviewed was 34 – eight black and 26 white women. Brief details
of each woman's life are given in Appendix 2.

During the course of writing this book I also visited a number of
places and people connected with women in, and after, prison:
HMP Holloway; HMP East Sutton Park; the Home Office Prison
Department; Wolverhampton probation service; Women In Pris-
on; Women In Special Hospitals; the Creative And Supportive
Trust; the Women Prisoners' Resource Centre (NACRO) and
New Careers Training, Camden (also NACRO).

3 *Interviews and after*

During the initial telephone call I explained that I was interested in the ways in which women had changed or rebuilt their lives after prison. On meeting each woman I reiterated that and, again, assured her of anonymity in the final written account. The interviews were loosely structured and focused on three areas of the woman's life: life before prison; life during prison; and life after prison. Most interviews lasted between 60 and 90 minutes but some were much longer. With three women there was a second interview. All the interviews, except the one conducted in a pub, were taped.

During the interviews the women spoke freely of their experience. Often this resurrected painful memories of dismissal and denial. In telling her story, the woman was gaining a recognition of her suffering. Yet such telling is painful. Commenting on this Sandy said:

> People come and listen to you and go away and leave you having dredged it all up. You don't get any feedback from that a lot of the time, you know. And it is very wearing. You relive it again. It's different if you're changing things because of it, that's different, but you still don't feel happy.

This presents the researcher with both short-term and long-term obligations. In the short term it is important that one does not leave the interviewee in a state of distress. As the interviews came to an end I would try to focus on the more positive aspects of the woman's life. Follow-up phone calls and visits may also be necessary to explore and come to terms with the experiences and the feelings that the interview raised. The interviewer should not simply walk away.

In the longer term the researcher has an obligation to let the researched know what has happened to her story. The expectation that such research can have recognizable and immediate results is overoptimistic and the researcher may need to present the final product (book, article, etc.) in a broader context, as part of an ongoing project aimed at a better understanding of one aspect of women's lives. It is important, both at the time of the fieldwork and later, that the interviewees be seen as co-workers with the researcher, rather than a resource to be exploited.

Most of the women said that they enjoyed the interview. Many of those who found it painful at times also said that they were pleased to have had the opportunity of re-examining their experiences. For some the pain suffered would be rendered useful if others could benefit from these experiences.

4 *Analysis*

The taped interviews were transcribed and the women's names changed along with any identifying details of place. The taped interviews were read and reread many times. Initially I looked for accounts of change and the circumstances surrounding change. From the transcripts I located the recurring themes of exclusion and inclusion in the lives of the women, and the themes of redirection, recognition and reciprocal relationships as they struggled to take charge of their lives. These are the themes which structure the written presentation and analysis of the women's experiences. The themes of exclusion and inclusion are taken from Foucault's (1991) account of the way in which contemporary society disciplines its members. The themes of redirection, recognition and reciprocal relationships arise within the women's accounts, but that of reciprocal relationships draws on the ideas put forward by Gilligan (1982) when she contrasts relationships based on hierarchy with those based on equality within a network.

There is a tension involved in writing of the experiences of women who have been so open about their lives and their feelings. Each woman gives her account from her own perspective. It was then necessary for me to situate that account within my own perspective. In the final account I have tried to differentiate between the women's accounts and my critique. Where there is a contradiction between the two perspectives I have tried to portray this. Respect for the woman involves presenting her account, but respect for all who co-operated and for future readers demands that I say what I see.

APPENDIX 2
ALICE AND 33 OTHER
WOMEN AFTER PRISON

This work is based on interviews with 34 women. The majority (30) had been out of prison for over two years. Their sentences ranged from six months to 15 years. Their offences may be grouped as follows:

Theft and fraud	11
Drug related	10
Violence	5
Political protest	4
Other	4

There were 26 white women and 8 black women. Their ages ranged from 22 to 82. Seventeen of the women were mothers, ten had children living with them at the time of the interview. Eight of these mothers were single parents. The current occupations of the 33 women (excluding Alice) are as follows:

Full-time employment	16
Full-time education	4
Part-time employment	2
Retired	1
Unemployed	
registered disabled	2
drug dependent	2

intending to continue
   education   2
with young children   2
other   2

At the time of the interviews none of the women was homeless.
The interviews were conducted between November 1990 and May
1991.

The 33 women and their stories

*In full-time employment working with prisoners and
ex-prisoners*

Collette is 32. She left prison in 1984 having completed her third
sentence. Each sentence was for an offence involving the defrauding of large amounts of money which she used to fund a heroin
habit.

Collette was nine when her mother died, and her father's two
subsequent marriages were unhappy. Her brother began offending
shortly after the mother's death, and was continually in and out of
prison. Collette became pregnant when she was 15. She left school
and the child was adopted. Collette began full-time employment as
a clerk and was eventually responsible for large amounts of
money. At 17 she left home and fell in love with a man who was
addicted to heroin. Thus began a lifestyle involving the use of
illegal drugs and the necessity for large amounts of money. It is
Collette's proud boast that she has been in employment for most
of her adult life. Indeed, two of her sentences involved the defrauding of an employer, the third involved the defrauding of the
DHSS.

Collette now lives alone in her own flat rented from a housing
association. She finds satisfaction in constructing a life for herself
and helping others to do so.

> Seeing the girls from Holloway and looking at them the way I
> was when I was about to get out, and watching them grow
> from that – its just the biggest buzz that any drug could ever
> have given me.

Paula is 44. She left prison in 1984 having served one year of a
two-and-a-half-year sentence for the importation of cannabis. It
was her first offence.

Paula was born in Jamaica, where she lived with her grandmother. From the age of 14 she visited her mother in London. At
17 she came to live with her mother and stepfather. She found her
stepfather too restrictive on her freedom and in order to leave
home she married at 18. The marriage lasted less than a year, but
she soon remarried. The second marriage lasted seven years. At 27
she was divorced with three children to support and her mother
living nearby.

> I was a single mother with children but I was happy. I was
> working, my mother was helping me to childmind the chil-
> dren. I wanted to have a kind of independence that you
> couldn't have without financial security. So I had a full-time
> job, I had two part-time jobs. It was work, work, work.

On a visit to Jamaica, she was given a present of a carved figure
which, on her return home, she discovered contained cannabis. She
arranged to import and sell more cannabis and was caught on her
second trip. She was given a two-and-a-half-year sentence but was
released on parole after a year. For Paula the impact of prison was
intensified by the impact on her family.

> The sentence affected me emotionally, but it affected my chil-
> dren physically, mentally, every way. Also my mother, be-
> cause she had to take on that responsibility. It wasn't just a
> question of I sentence *you* to prison.

Cara, aged 29, left prison in 1987 having served one year of a
two-year sentence for the importation of cannabis. She had one
previous offence, of shoplifting, as a juvenile.

Cara describes her childhood as happy. On leaving school she
had difficulty finding work and became involved in the selling of
pictures, door to door. Since this was not declared for tax or insurance, the whole venture was illegal. At this time Cara was living
with a man and became pregnant. The relationship ended shortly
after the birth of her daughter. She became very depressed and
accepted a friend's invitation of a weekend in London to cheer her
up. Enchanted by life in London, Cara asked her mother to take
care of the baby while she found a flat and a job. During this time
she became aware that her friend was involved in not only using
cannabis but also importing it. Her friend was arrested and needed
money to pay urgent debts. She eventually persuaded Cara to
make a journey to Jamaica to bring back some cannabis to sell.
Cara was arrested on her return and held on remand for three

weeks. During this time she learned that her daughter had been made a ward of court by the father. Despite being told of the likely outcome she was shocked by her sentence.

> Even though my solicitor had said to me 'You're going to prison', I didn't believe it. I was working. I had a job, and I thought 'They know it's a one-off, there's no point in sentencing me to prison'.

Cara is now living with her daughter in her own flat rented from a housing association.

Lisa is 31. She left prison in 1991 having served three years and three months of a four-year sentence for armed robbery.

Lisa never knew her father. The first seven years of her life were spent with her mother and grandmother. Then her mother married a West Indian and had five children in seven years. Lisa found the situation difficult. She was embarrassed by being part of a mixed family. She began to truant from school, shoplift and run away from home. At 14 she was taken into care and experienced a number of children's homes before she was fostered at 15. She describes the family as 'really nice' but she felt that she did not fit in. At 16 she was living in a bedsitter with her boyfriend and working in a sandwich business, taking orders by telephone. That job lasted three months; it was Lisa's only experience of paid employment until the present. She became pregnant and had a daughter. The father had become involved in petty theft and was sent to prison. Lisa and her daughter were living on an estate in the East End of London. There it was easy to dispose of stolen goods. Lisa began to shoplift on a large scale. At 19 she received nine months' borstal training. She placed her daughter in voluntary care. On release they both spent five months in a hostel and were then rehoused. By this time Lisa had begun a relationship with another man. She became pregnant again and married the father. He was becoming involved in serious crime. At this stage in her life, aged 25, she was introduced to heroin. At first she and her husband used it occasionally. But eventually she became addicted, just as he received a seven-year sentence for armed robbery. Throughout this period Lisa had been involved in shoplifting, but never enough to be imprisoned. She had been given probation orders and suspended sentences. However, the heroin addiction required large amounts of money. Lisa became involved in armed robbery. She was arrested and sentenced to four years' imprisonment. Because of her behaviour in prison she served most of this sentence.

Fran is 46. She left prison in 1975 having served 16 months of a two-year sentence for fraud. Prior to that she had served two sentences of six months which she had accepted as the price to be paid for her life as a professional criminal. For Fran this was a life which she had freely chosen and which afforded excitement and style. However, the attractions of the life began to pall. Even before her final sentence she had begun to question the patterns and attitudes that had structured her activities. She began to recognize the importance of personal relationships which validated the non-criminal aspects of her life. During her last sentence she felt estranged from many of the conventions that had previously governed her life among the criminalized. She became concerned to make a positive contribution to society. Fran is now working on behalf of criminalized women. She is committed to reducing the estrangement and brutality that women experience in prison, and ultimately to the total abolition of prison.

Meg is now 52. She left prison in 1986, having served ten and a half years for murder. Meg still says she was innocent, and at the time of the trial a petition was presented to the Home Office, signed by over 300 local people who believed she was innocent.

At the time of her conviction Meg had three sons, aged 14, 12 and nine, and a two-year-old daughter. The separation from all her children was traumatic for Meg, and she feels that she has really lost her daughter's childhood.

On leaving prison, Meg returned to her home town and began to re-establish herself. Although she is now divorced, she is on good terms with her ex-husband, and she is also on good terms with her children, with whom she has had to re-establish relationships. Her extended family has been supportive and she has found good neighbours. This was particularly important when Meg became a target of press harassment by journalists intent on resurrecting a scandal.

At first work was difficult to find. Meg has had employment in a number of factories. Through this she has managed to furnish a home. Now she works full-time and is committed to enabling women who come out of prison to take charge of their lives and learn to value themselves

> The time in prison, the traumas you go through after, I can relate to all of that. Although I'm working and I'm able to support myself and I'm getting a home together, I'm also feeding my soul. I don't feel that all these ten years were totally wasted. I feel that I can now give a lot more than I could've done had I not experienced that.

Now she is also an important part of her children's lives again. She can give financial assistance and emotional support to them.

And that's feeding me, feeding my soul for all the years that I sat in prison and literally ate my stomach away [in prison, Meg suffered from stomach ulcers] because I couldn't be their mum and I couldn't provide for them, I'm being able to do it now. And it's mending, it's healing me.

Laura is 25. In 1987 she was given a six-month sentence for a first offence involving credit card fraud, deception and handling stolen goods valued at £4,500. Six months after leaving prison she was remanded in custody, on similar charges, for five and a half weeks. When that case came to court, Laura was given a community service order.

Laura grew up with three brothers and both parents. She describes herself as disruptive and rebellious at school, and she was expelled from her first secondary school. On leaving school at 16, with a CSE Grade 1 in English, she went to work in an office. At this time her friends had criminal records and were involved in criminal activities. Through a boyfriend she acquired a stolen cheque book and credit card. She also began to supplement her income by drug dealing:

Marijuana, and a bit of LSD and sulphate, stuff like that.

However, an encounter with a friend took her to Narcotics Anonymous and she began to question her lifestyle. At this point she was arrested and given a custodial sentence. Six months later she had started an education course and was making plans for the future when she succumbed to temptation – she had no money and someone offered her a stolen credit card. She was arrested on first using it. Although she was initially remanded in custody, Laura was eventually given a community service order which she served at CAST. This not only allowed her to pay the assigned penalty for her offence, but also gave her the opportunity of working with others to change her life for the better.

Laura, however, comments on the capriciousness of sentencing:

This is my second offence and I'm glad I didn't go to prison, but it just showed the system for what it is. There's no consistency. For my first offence I get six months. You know I had brilliant mitigation for that first offence when I went to court. I'd got a job and really changed. The second offence they gave me community service.

In other full-time employment

Rene is 32. She now runs her own business, a children's toy shop in South London. She is married with four children, a boy aged 16 and three girls aged 11, 10 and two. At the time of the interview Rene had been out of prison for just over two years, having left in 1988. She had served 14 months for using a stolen cheque book. It was her third offence and her second prison sentence.

Rene was nine years old when her parents left the country and she and her sister were put into the care of the local authority. Their first placement was with a white foster mother in an area in which they felt conspicuous as the only black children. The placement was not successful and Rene was separated from her sister and lived with a succession of relatives. At 15 she was living with an older friend when she was arrested for shoplifting and sent to an assessment centre. The centre recommended that she be given a place at an approved school but she was then pregnant and so was allowed to stay at a children's home where she was happy. On the birth of her son she began work while the home staff took care of the child. Within a year she was arrested for theft, remanded in custody and so lost her job. When the case came to court she was fined. She still maintains that she was not guilty of that offence.

At 18 she had her own flat and she also had friends who were using stolen cheque books. She followed their example and was caught. She was given a six month prison sentence. On leaving prison she continued to use stolen cheque books and, coming to court again, she was given a probation order. She found the probation officer helpful in providing emotional support and practical assistance.

When the probation order was finished she began to reoffend and was eventually arrested and held on remand. During this time Rene discovered she was pregnant again. Her child was born while she was on remand and she had to take the new baby into the prison. The impact of this, and the effect on her other children, made Rene determined not to return to prison, and to avoid crime.

Rene drew up a business plan and borrowed money from her father and from the bank (the bank is unaware of her convictions). She is now established in her own shop and takes pride in the local reaction to her enterprise.

Susan is 43 and employed as a secretary. She is also on probation. Her employers are unaware of her history of convictions. She last left prison in 1984.

Susan was adopted at six months and she feels that this has

influenced her behaviour. As a child she had a compulsion to steal small items of little value. Later as an adult she began to defraud employers of large sums of money. Her first court appearance was in 1971 at the age of 24, when she was charged with the theft of £1500 from her employer. She was given a custodial sentence of six months. Her next court appearance was in 1979 when she felt her life to be in chaos because her marriage was breaking down. She was given a community service order of 120 hours. She worked as a home help and enjoyed the experience. Community service is, she feels, underused.

> You still have loss of liberty because your whole week has to revolve around your community service, but you're doing something good, and at the same time, society doesn't have to pay the price for getting you back into society, because you never leave it.

She subsequently received a nine-month suspended sentence which was activated when in 1984 she received a 15-month sentence. She then served eight months of the two years and was given parole. Compared to her first sentence, this sentence was served in conditions which were designed to ameliorate the exclusion that characterizes the experience of imprisonment. Susan was in an open prison and prisoners were allowed out to visit local people and places of interest. Leaving prison in these circumstances proved less traumatic.

> It was much more like reality. We used to go out three times a week. It wasn't as though we weren't used to sitting in people's houses, and talking to ordinary people and going in cars.

A year prior to the interview Susan had once again been charged with deception and remanded in custody. However, on appearing at court she was given a two-year probation order and she feels that this is appropriate. She has decided that she is unlikely to reoffend because she has had the opportunity of assessing her situation. The problems around her adoption have been resolved by meeting her 'birth' family, whom she disliked. She considers that she was fortunate to be adopted. She now no longer feels the need to steal. As well as being in paid employment, Susan works as a volunteer for a national charity.

Bernice is 37 and served eighteen months of a two-year sentence (1977–9) for the importation of cannabis. She is now working with deprived children, but has not declared her conviction. She lives with her husband and four-year-old son in their flat in West London. Bernice grew up on a sheep station in Australia. She was one of five daughters and was particularly close to her father. Throughout her childhood she was aware of her father's excessive drinking but it was only during her early adult years that his alcoholism began to threaten his livelihood. Her mother was very worried and depressed about the situation but would not allow Bernice to confront the father, fearing repercussions. Bernice trained as a teacher and eventually left Australia to travel overland to Europe via Asia. In Asia she discovered cannabis and decided this was the solution to all problems, since it induced euphoria without the violence associated with alcohol. She became peripherally involved in the smuggling of three kilos from Afghanistan to India. This eventually found its way to Britain, and when the crime was discovered her name was given as a part of the chain. Bernice was, by then, in England where she was questioned and subsequently arrested. She received a three-year sentence. She was surprised at the lack of opportunity for rehabilitation in prison. Since leaving prison she has had to keep her conviction secret to obtain work in fields in which she feels she can be useful.

Beatrice is 82. She left prison in 1969 having served six months of a nine-month sentence for kidnapping. She is a qualified medical practitioner and is still active in child therapy.

Beatrice tells how she was born into the British upper class, into a family of wealth and privilege. She has spent most of her life distancing herself from this background. Her prison sentence was the result of her insisting on her right to keep a child who had been given into her care by his father. Prison, she insists, was unable to affect her greatly because she was cushioned by her social status.

Beatrice says that she lost nothing by the experience. Her work continued. Her income was unaffected. Her friends were, like her, rebels within society. The real restriction on her life came later, from a loss of money from which her freedom was derived:

I have been bankrupt and that's much worse, much worse. Bankruptcy was really painful, worse than prison. That altered my whole momentum.

Wanda, aged 39, is practising as an aromatherapist. She has served a number of custodial sentences for offences related to drug abuse and theft. Her last sentence finished in 1985.

Wanda was born to an Irish chambermaid and put into a

children's home at birth. At nine years old she was adopted and her name was changed. She has since taken back her original name. Six months after the adoption both parents died, one of cancer, the other of a heart attack. Wanda went to live with other members of the family but was ill-treated and returned to care. Her behaviour at school was disruptive, and at times violent. She was sent to an approved school. From the age of ten she was given large doses of Largactyl. At 14 she was given electroconvulsive therapy. At 15 she was remanded in Holloway and there she spent her sixteenth birthday. Her first custodial sentence was ten months' borstal training. This she enjoyed and did not want to leave when her time was over.

Since that time Wanda has been involved in petty crime and drug abuse. She had a series of jobs but nothing lasted because of the disruptive lifestyle. She charts a real change in her life from her attendance at a residential drug rehabilitation programme. She stayed there for two years. Subsequently she trained as an aromatherapist. Wanda now struggles to fit into a social world very different to the ones she has known.

Peggy is 52. She left prison in 1983 having served one prison sentence of four months for running a disorderly house.

Peggy was a prostitute who specialized in domination and had a regular clientele. She is convinced that the police had a grudge against her because previous attempts to bring cases against her had proved unsuccessful. In this case she insists that the evidence was fabricated as officers gave false testimony. Since the case she has continued to work but only as a prostitute's maid, as the police seem intent on further prosecution.

While she was in prison Peggy encountered no hostility. The consensus of opinion expressed by officers and inmates was that she had done no harm and ought not to be there. However, as a result of the sentence she was unable to pay her mortgage and she lost her home. She is now rehoused in a flat belonging to a housing association.

Martha is 25 years old and works for a small human rights lobbying organization. She was a member of the Greenham Common peace camp and involved in politically motivated crime. She has been in prison seven times, three times on remand, and four times serving a sentence. Of the four sentences three were for short periods as the result of refusing to pay a fine. Her last sentence was for four months, without any option. She served two months in 1988.

There's such a difference between being in for not paying a fine and you know you can pay that and get out if you're totally desperate and you know there is somebody out there with money to do it.

For Martha, as for the other women from Greenham, prison was part of the choice made when she decided to live at the camp and become involved in actions involving obstruction, criminal damage and sabotage. As a schoolgirl of 16 she had visited the camp and determined to live there. She joined the camp at 18, having already left home.

Barbara is 50. She, too, was a member of the Greenham Common peace camp. She left prison in 1985, having served a sentence of four months. Prior to that she had served a number of shorter sentences for refusing to pay a fine. All the offences were related to activities organized by members of the peace camp.

Barbara was a wife and mother when she first visited Greenham Common in 1981. Prior to that she had been a member of CND, but had wanted to do more. In the years that followed Barbara became more involved, staying at the camp for longer periods but never living there full-time.

I kept going back and forth from home and staying there about 10 days and going home for a couple of weeks. One thing led to another and from obstructing traffic – we did feel that was dangerous and the police were becoming quite violent – we started cutting down fences, which seemed less violent somehow. I felt very strongly about cruise missiles being there so that was the reason I went along.

Prison made Barbara question further the standards by which much of life is conducted. There she encountered women whose poverty and victimization had resulted in custodial sentences.

The other women who are in prison are political prisoners really because the reasons they're in prison are because they are poor. The people who should be in prison are those people making weapons of mass destruction. There are these institutions showing people how to kill. If you've got a real reason for killing somebody, maybe this man has been beating you up all your life, you need punishment. I think it's all hypocritical.

Barbara is now working for a women's refuge.

Judith, aged 30, is the third woman involved in Greenham Common activities. She served a number of short sentences for refusing to pay fines, the last one in 1983.

Judith left home when she was 16 and worked in a bank. With the bank she moved to London, where she had her own flat. She left the bank to work for a voluntary sector organization. For two years Judith combined a part-time job, as a development worker, with living at Greenham Common. She spent half the week in London and half the week in Greenham. Her decision to go to prison rather than pay a fine arose from her feelings of solidarity with the other Greenham women, and of indignation with a system that would not allow her to protest.

> Other women were going to prison but I did have the money to pay, because I was working, but I didn't believe that I should pay to exercise my right to protest. I didn't believe that I should have to pay for freedom of speech.

Her experience in prison led her to work voluntarily for WIP. She is now employed by a local authority play scheme.

In full-time education

Nicki, now aged 26, was born in the North of England into a working-class family. Throughout her childhood she was abused by her father. Her persistent offending brought her before the courts and eventually, to her relief, she went into care at the age of 12. Her offending continued. She absconded several times. She was charged with breaking and entering, and theft. After care the offending continued and she became involved in drug use. She returned to a college of further education and was doing GCE O levels when she first visited Greenham Common. Her visits became longer and more frequent and she eventually went to live there instead of pursuing A-level courses at college.

While at Greenham, Nicki became involved in much political action but imprisonment presented her with a dilemma most noticeable during her last and longest sentence. This was in 1988 when she served two months of a four month sentence. Although she had been sentenced as a Greenham woman she felt that her sympathies and sense of identification were with the other prisoners sharing her background of institutional care, petty crime and drug abuse. Prison seemed inevitable. She determined to break this pattern. Before her final sentence she had enrolled at a residential college of further education for women. The course was disrupted by the prison sentence but she received much support from tutors and fellow students. She applied to, and was accepted by, an Oxbridge college.

Terri is 23 and is living at a project set up for ex-offenders in full-time education. She is following short courses at a local college of further education prior to taking an access course to qualify for an undergraduate place. Terri left prison in 1990, having served three years of a seven-year sentence after being found guilty of the manslaughter of her youngest child.

Terri lived in East London in a working-class family. At 16 she left home to live with a man who proved to be violent. Her first child was born when she was 17 and her second child a year later. Terri was suffering from post-natal depression and was heavily tranquillized. Her ten-month-old baby died of neglect. Her elder son was put into care, and fostered by people who now want to adopt him.

Because of the nature of her offence, Terri suffered physical and verbal abuse from other prisoners and served her sentence on Rule 43. As a young woman already depressed, and further traumatized by the results of her actions, she spent long periods in isolation with only books for company.

On leaving prison, Terri was advised by her probation officer to change her name and not admit to her offence. For her the stigma is more than that of ex-prisoner:

> You always feel as though you are holding something back. What's the alternative? Losing your friends?

Bella is 31. In 1983 when she was 23 she stabbed a woman to death and was charged with manslaughter. She spent four and a half years in Broadmoor, and two years in the secure unit of a psychiatric hospital. Since then she has been living in the community in a council flat. Bella is following an access course leading to a degree programme at a local polytechnic. She also works as a volunteer at a drop-in centre for the homeless.

Bella describes her childhood as unhappy. Her father was violent to her, her three sisters and her mother. At school Bella was unpopular and was teased by other children. She used to steal small items and when teachers told her parents she received further beatings.

At 18 Bella left home and became a residential care worker. She was successful and promoted to senior care worker. Her personal

relationships were unhappy. Her parents left the UK and she lived
with different members of the family. The situations were never
satisfactory. She became involved with a number of violent men.
When she was 21 she met someone who seemed different. To him
she confided the sad story of her life. She then began to receive
phone calls from a woman, taunting her with details of her life and
telling her to stay away from the man. She began to feel ill. She
stopped eating and could not sleep. She felt afraid of the woman
and the woman's family. Eventually she went to see the woman,
taking a knife for protection. There was a fight and the woman
died. Bella cannot remember the details of the event.

Bella is highly critical of the brutality which she observed and
experienced on C1 in Holloway and in Broadmoor. She also recognizes that there were individuals who showed compassion and who
helped her to recover. Now she faces the frustration of an after-
care regime to which she is subject and which she finds inadequate.
In one year she has had four different psychiatrists:

> I find it hard to get used to someone, especially if you have to
> tell him about your sexual life, because that's what they want
> to know. You pour out your whole life in 20 minutes and then
> they're gone.

For her the real support comes from friends, from her boyfriend
who listens and understands, and from her women friends who
keep in contact.

Kathy is 52. She left prison in 1979 having served three years of a
five-year sentence for fraud. The charge arose from white-collar
crime within her own business. Having begun to explore the possibility of fraud, Kathy became involved in more complicated and
lucrative schemes and found these exciting. The money she made
allowed her to sustain an extravagant lifestyle and she found she
was mixing with other successful criminals. However, to her close
friends she kept secret the criminal activities of her business. On
reflection, Kathy says she was not happy despite the consumption
of goods, alcohol and drugs with which she filled her time and
spent her money. She became careless and was caught.

In prison Kathy was amazed by the poverty of other women's
lives and by the strength with which they endured. She also began
to learn more about herself through education. On leaving prison
Kathy continued her education. She became critical not only of the
prison system but also of the prevailing political and social structures and the part that she had previously played in these:

I went in a Tory voter and real establishment. I had never challenged the status quo except by my actions, but in a way that wasn't a challenge, it was stepping over a line. It seemed a logical progression. I was still feeling part of the system, I was just doing it better than anyone else.

Since leaving prison, Kathy has made a significant contribution to the work of two voluntary organizations which provide the space and the structures within which women ex-prisoners can gain the confidence and skills to take a place within society. Kathy is now retraining, so that she, too, can move away from her prison past and make a contribution in another context.

In part-time employment

Olive is 33. She lives in a council flat with her two children, aged two and a half years and four months. She left prison in 1986, having served two years and nine months of a four-year sentence for supplying a small amount of cocaine for the personal use of an acquaintance.

Olive describes her childhood as 'difficult' and her early adult life as 'chaotic'. She finds her middle-class family are still overcritical and suspicious of her. At the time of the offence Olive was living with a wealthy man. They were both involved in the recreational use of cocaine. Someone asked Olive to obtain some and she was caught in the act of supplying it. It was her first offence; she had never before appeared in court.

For Olive the experience of prison was one of waste and boredom. She became very depressed. On leaving prison she looked for therapy. Impressed by the people at a Jungian centre, Olive was unable to meet even the reduced fees. She has decided that therapy is something that she needs in order fully to understand herself and her life but it is something that must wait until she has a better income. In the meantime she has had some counselling, which she found useful.

Olive very much enjoys her daughters and devotes much time and attention to them. She combines this with work from home. In the future she hopes to take a degree at the local polytechnic. She would like to become a primary school teacher but fears that her record may make her unacceptable.

Beverley is 27. She has a two-month-old son and she looks after a neighbour's three-year-old daughter in her West London council flat. Beverley completed her fourth prison sentence in 1988, when she served three months for assaulting a prison officer during her previous sentence. She has faced a number of charges relating to theft, fraud and assault.

When she was seven years old, Beverley was sent to a special school for children with learning difficulties. She felt out of place and began to truant and behave disruptively, until she was eventually expelled. No other place was found for her and her home tutor lasted for only a short time. From the age of 13 Beverley had no schooling. She spent her days wandering about the area. She began shoplifting. On her sixteenth birthday she began her first prison sentence for shoplifting. Six months later she left prison and moved out of her parents' house to a hostel. There she stayed until she was 19 and was given her own flat. During this time she had committed a number of offences and had served her second sentence for shoplifting and assaulting a police officer. Throughout her sentences Beverley was an uncooperative prisoner. At 23 she served a full twelve months of a twelve month sentence for defrauding mail order companies. During this time her violent behaviour resulted in her assignment to C1 (the psychiatric unit) of Holloway. It was here that her probation officer introduced her to the welfare worker from WIP. Through this worker Beverley found a flat and the help that she needed in dealing with the frustrations in her life. She kept in touch on leaving prison and still speaks of the people at WIP as

nice people and you can speak to them and they can help you.

For Beverley, having the responsibility of her own child has made her determined not to reoffend, while the trust shown by the neighbour who leaves her child with Beverley has endorsed her decision.

Disabled

Jo is 52. In 1985 she was released after having spent the preceding 16 years in special hospitals, first Broadmoor and then Rampton. This was the result of a court appearance for the possession of dangerous drugs, following a suicide attempt. Following this she attacked a fellow prisoner who stole her tobacco and then taunted her. Her manner, her actions and her failure to provide an articulate explanation led to her losing her liberty for an indefinite period.

Jo is the daughter of a violent and mentally unstable woman.

Throughout her childhood Jo suffered frequent beatings. She was never able to please her mother. However, it was in an attempt to help her mother, then in a psychiatric hospital, that Jo ran away to Scotland in a vain search for her natural father. To make the journey she stole from her employers and thus began a cycle of prosecution and imprisonment, followed by homelessness and petty crime to ensure further imprisonment to provide food and shelter.

Within prison Jo found herself experiencing emotional reactions of a strength which frightened her, but she did not know how to explain this, or to whom she should explain it. She gained a reputation as a violent and aggressive prisoner. Eventually she was sent to Broadmoor for the first time.

On leaving Broadmoor she found work in a service station and was introduced to 'uppers' to keep awake during double shifts. She then began to take 'downers' to sleep on days off. Jo was arrested and sent to a psychiatric hospital under a probation order. There she was introduced to heroin by a fellow patient. Thus began a long addiction leading to an attempted suicide. When she was found she was in possession of heroin and she was sent to Broadmoor for the second time. She feels that it was only in the last two years of her incarceration that she began to make any progress towards change. It was then that she met a psychiatrist and a psychologist who gained her confidence, and with them she began to re-examine her life.

Jo is now a member of WISH and is concerned to publicize the condition of many women within the special hospitals. She also provides support for women facing a court appearance which might result in their allocation to a special hospital. She is registered disabled because of arthritis.

Sandy is 52. She left prison in 1985 having served three and a half years for illegal burial and defrauding the DHSS. Two of three years were spent in the maximum security wing for women, Durham H Wing.

After leaving boarding school, Sandy spent her early working life in the army and had been a military policewoman. In Foucauldian terms she had certainly been subject to discipline. However, Sandy had not become an acceptable disciplined subject. She lived with her mother, her lesbian lover and her lover's mother, and ran an animal sanctuary. Suffering from a chronic disease, Sandy is registered disabled. The income on which the women lived and ran the sanctuary was limited to two old age pensions, one disablement allowance and one social security benefit. The death of the lover's mother posed problems. It was decided to bury the body and keep drawing the pension. On discovery all were prosecuted and convicted. On appeal Sandy's mother was released.

In prison Sandy continued to defy the disciplinary society. Her reputation as a difficult prisoner resulted in her transfer to Durham H Wing. Designed for category A women prisoners, of whom there are usually only two or three, Durham H Wing has 36 places, and the other places are filled by women doing longer sentences or who are thought difficult to control. Thus these women are held in conditions of unusual and unnecessary severity. This is a prison within a prison, with very little natural light, subject to continual surveillance. The women there are objects of hatred by the men in the rest of the jail. These men believe that the women of Durham are exceptionally malevolent and let it be known that their food, prepared by the men, has also been contaminated by them.

Sandy still lives with the legacy of Durham. Her eyesight has deteriorated because of the constant artificial lighting. Her teeth have been permanently damaged by prison dentistry. Her chronic condition has been made worse by the refusal of the authorities at Durham to recognize that she was unfit for heavy work. When she was transferred to Askham Grange at the end of her sentence this was recognized and in fact she spent most of her time at Askham Grange in the hospital wing.

Sandy is convinced that Durham H Wing is a cruel and unnecessary part of the criminal justice system.

Retired

Doris, aged 73, is Sandy's mother. Doris was 64 when she was sentenced to one year's imprisonment for illegal burial and defrauding the DHSS. She was freed on appeal after serving four months in 1981.

Doris now lives in an old people's home where no one knows her secret. She is anxious that it is not discovered. Because of the notoriety surrounding her trial one of her sons has disowned her.

Unemployed

Linda is 42 and has been out of prison since 1984. She is a registered drug addict who uses heroin daily. She lives in a housing association flat which has been her home since leaving prison.

Prior to her last offence Linda had faced a number of charges and spent time in prisons and mental hospitals because of her drug addiction and activities related to maintaining her supply.

Linda was born in a small village in the West Country. She saw her mother occasionally but lived with foster parents. She was abused by her foster brother. At 14 the foster parents decided that she was beyond their control and she was sent to live with her mother. Her mother, too, was unable to control Linda, who was then sent to an approved school. There Linda learned, from the other girls, about the possibilities of excitement and money in London's West End. At 15 she ran away to Soho and began using heroin. The heroin addiction led Linda to prostitution as a means of supporting a habit. Possession of heroin was a further cause of court appearances.

Linda feels that the cycle of court appearances and prison is now broken because of a probation officer who listened to what she wanted and was prepared to allow her to articulate her own needs and plan her response. That officer also found Linda's flat, her first home of her own. Linda now feels that she has some control over her life. She will continue to use heroin and when she feels the need she will attend a detoxification centre. She no longer feels the need to pretend that she wants to give up.

Norma is 34. Prior to the interview in January 1991 she had been remanded in Holloway but on coming to trial she was given a two-year probation order. Her offence, like her many previous offences, was related to her drug addiction. She had been using stolen cheques to fund her habit. Norma's last prison sentence ended in June 1986 after her baby was born dead. Extensive campaigning by WIP and the National Council for Civil Liberties resulted in the exercise of the royal prerogative of mercy.

Norma grew up in a working-class family in one of the poorer districts of a northern city. Both Norma and her two brothers proved too difficult for their parents. All three were involved in juvenile delinquency. Norma was sent to an approved school at 12, when her parents could no longer control her. By the time she was 16 she was addicted to heroin and had begun the series of offences of shoplifting and cheque fraud by which she found the money to buy the drug.

In 1981, when she was pregnant with her first child, Norma came off heroin. However, shortly after the birth she was remanded in custody. The baby went to live with Norma's mother and has remained there.

Norma's second child was expected during a sentence which she was serving in Holloway. Because of complications with the earlier pregnancy, she was being kept under observation by the hospital and attending for regular check-ups. Two weeks before the expected birth a new medical officer was appointed to the prison and cancelled outside hospital appointments. Norma was a week past her due date when she complained of pains. She was given Algipan to rub on her back. By 2 a.m. the pain was worse and Norma woke Carole (see below) who was in her dormitory. They called the nurse who gave Norma a cursory examination, pronounced that the baby would be born that night or the next day, and removed Norma to a single cell. The pains continued. It was not until the next morning that she was taken to hospital. There the doctor said she should have come in some weeks earlier. The baby was born dead. The inquest pronounced a verdict of natural causes. Norma was released.

I came out to nothing. I had nowhere to live. I went out and I went straight back [on drugs]. Drugs were the first thing I looked for, which was just an escape really.

Mandy is 28. She left prison in 1988 and is optimistic about her future. She has a stable supportive relationship and a secure home. She intends to pursue her education.

Mandy describes her childhood as unsettled and unhappy. Her mother was extremely violent towards her and at 14 she was raped by her uncle. Her early life left its mark. She experienced outbursts of violence and found herself in a series of relationships with violent men. Her appearances in court on charges of drunkenness, criminal damage and arson were symptoms of the chaos she felt within. Mandy looked forward to her first prison sentence in the hope that she would be helped to do something about a life that she felt was out of control. She was disappointed. On remand prior to her second prison sentence Mandy changed her plea to 'not guilty' in order to spend Christmas in Holloway. She had nowhere else to go and Holloway provided a community, shelter and food. Rules were relaxed, cells were unlocked, movement was less restricted. Mandy enjoyed that Christmas.

After leaving home at 16, Mandy experienced a range of hostels for the homeless in London. Her record as an arsonist made her unwelcome at many. Her violent behaviour resulted in her leaving others.

However, Mandy's life has changed. For the past two years she has lived with the same friend in privately rented accommodation and for five years she has also found support at WIP. Here she works as a volunteer and this gives her access to a member of the staff who acts as a counsellor and guide. Mandy recognizes that not only do these people help her, but also that she has something to give.

Hazel is 35. She left prison in 1988, having served 17 months for possession of cocaine and cannabis, with intent to supply. Hazel is now living with her 11-year-old daughter and planning to continue her education.

Hazel was a young mother living on social security when she was first introduced to drug use.

> Out of curiosity I tried it and I liked it. Then I got involved as a way to make money. It was easy money. I just used to take a little bit now and then and, as the years went on, I just got more and more into it.

By the time she was arrested, Hazel was addicted. She began her sentence in Holloway and was then transferred to Bulwood Hall. While at Bulwood Hall she began to pursue her education. She took courses in secretarial skills and then did a course which involved leaving the prison daily to work with deprived children. For nine months she left the prison on weekdays at 8 a.m. and returned at 7 p.m. She was not accompanied by a guard. During this time she began to meet the welfare worker from WIP on a regular basis. Hazel felt that here was someone who understood her.

> You don't want to be sitting there and talking to someone who's never experienced. They don't know what you're going through, nobody knows what you're going through, only someone in that position.

Hazel now feels that she has re-evaluated her life and is determined to develop her own potential and provide support for her child.

Janice is 30. She left prison in 1989 having served 16 months of a two-year sentence for handling stolen goods. She lives on a council estate with her four children aged 11, eight, seven and five. She suffers from depression.

Apart from a caution for shoplifting when she was 13, Janice had no history of offending until she was 18. At that time she was arrested for shoplifting. At 21 she was involved in the use of stolen cheque books and cards. At 24 she served her first prison sentence for deception.

Janice is angry. She feels unable to cope with the demands of four lively children on the third floor of a block of flats. She fears reprisals from men who used to supply her with stolen cheque books. She has asked for a move, but to no avail. She finds the DSS staff unhelpful and provocative. When asked if she is likely to return to prison, Janice replies that she would not become involved in planned crime, but that she cannot guarantee that her frustration with officialdom will not erupt into violence and an assault on a person or damage to property.

Carole is 37. She left prison in 1987, having served 26 months of a 30-month sentence for supplying heroin. Her husband, who was more involved in the enterprise, is still serving his ten-year sentence at Dartmoor. Carole lives with two of her daughters, aged 11 and five. The five-year-old was born during Carole's time in prison. Carole's eldest daughter, aged 16, has left home but still visits regularly.

Carole grew up in the Lake District with her grandmother. She gained a college place but left at 19 to come to London. By the time she was 21 she was pregnant and married to her current husband. Initially, he was involved in handling stolen goods. Carole became dependent on Valium and involved in shoplifting. Eventually he progressed to drug dealing and became addicted to heroin. When he was arrested for supplying heroin, Carole continued his business. She was arrested and sentenced to prison. Her two daughters went to live with her father in the North of England. Her youngest daughter was born in prison and stayed with her mother for the first year of her life.

Throughout her marriage Carole's husband has been violent towards her, assaulting her even on home leave from prison. From prison he writes threatening and abusive letters. Carole is torn. She cannot decide whether or not to divorce him. Before prison she was dependent on him. Now she knows she can cope without him.

> I've been able to do the things that I never thought I'd do –
> build a house up, look after my kids, stick up for myself. Plus
> I've met some good friends.

However, she feels guilty about serving divorce papers while he is still in prison. And she fears his response should she do so. The prospect of attacking him in anger and facing another prison sentence seems more acceptable to her than the calculated attempt to remove him from her life by recourse to judicial process.

Tracey is 22. She has been out of prison since 1990, having served three months for attempting to use stolen credit cards. She is currently unemployed and pregnant. She is living in a shared house provided by an organization which is committed to housing ex-prisoners.

Tracey is still very close to the rest of her family and receives much emotional and financial support from them, especially from her mother. On leaving school at 16, Tracey did a one-year course leading to a qualification as a care assistant. She then joined an agency and worked as a nanny. She is proud of the good references she has accumulated in the five years of this work.

At 19 Tracey left home and lived in her own flat. This was burgled and it was then that she found some credit cards in a phone box. Seeing an easy way to recoup the losses of the burglary, she attempted to use the cards and was caught. She was un-cooperative with the police and resisted a search. Later on remand in prison she resisted a search. For this, her first offence, she was eventually sentenced to three months.

Tracey now feels that her future career prospects as a nanny are blighted. She would have to declare her prison record and this would put her at a disadvantage. Since leaving prison she has had a number of jobs in catering, but she did not enjoy them. She is resentful at losing her place in society. She feels that the consequences of her prison sentence are out of all proportion to her original crime.

June is 38. She is currently unemployed but looking for work. In 1984 she left prison having served six months of a nine-month sentence for deception. Her previous sentence was for using credit cards which were delivered, by mistake, to her address. Both offences were related to her use of drugs.

At 19, June came to London to work on the stage. She met a writer, married him and has an 18-year-old son. Early in her marriage June became involved in drug use and was soon addicted to Mandrax. Her marriage ended. Throughout her life she has become addicted to a number of different drugs and has suffered several overdoses. She found it difficult to plan her life and was frequently in chaotic situations. Two years ago she suffered a severe overdose which left her temporarily paralysed in one leg. She then decided to attempt a residential rehabilitation programme. There ex-addicts worked with current addicts to examine their lives and personalities. June feels that this has been successful. If she can find work she will be able to stabilize her life and avoid the situations which have previously led to crime and prison.

APPENDIX 3
ALICE, ONE YEAR ON

Alice told me her story in January 1991. By December I had completed the work on which this book is based and had written the preceding chapters. I arranged to see Alice again to learn how she had fared during the year. She had fared well and was facing the future with confidence. As with the other women who had successfully changed their lives, one can see, in Alice's account, the interrelationship of the three factors necessary to this change: redirection, recognition and reciprocal relationships.

Alice had determined not to commit crime, to resist the suggestions of former associates and to discover the good in herself. To this end she ordered her life.

> I had two paid jobs. During the day I was doing secretarial work for this charity and six nights a week I worked in McDonald's. The other night I was doing a computer course.

Alice had no time for crime, or even for spending her money. By August she had enough money saved to accompany a friend who was visiting her family in St Lucia. The proposed two-week holiday became a two-month holiday.

> It was really therapeutic. I felt healthy and happy. I was laughing so much I felt confident enough to do anything.

On her return Alice learned that her former boyfriend had been trying to contact her. This was the man who had rejected her when she was last arrested, and whose rejection had caused her much distress. They are now reunited but have not re-established old patterns.

> We got back together but the relationship is different. I'm much more in control. I don't feel that I have to cling on to him or that he is seeing other women. We each have our own lives to lead and I'm not so emotionally dependent. He's more supportive, like a good friend.

Alice is now working for her boyfriend and is actively pursuing her plans to set up her own business. She has worked honestly at other relationships in her life, developing potential, recognizing, with pain, limitations and refusing to collude in rewritings of history.

> I see my brother regularly. He's still in Broadmoor but he's got a tribunal coming up soon. I've seen some of the reports they write about him. They say he's not intelligent, but he is. It's just that he says strange things or says things in strange ways. You have to really listen to him.
>
> My mother is confused. She's had two bad marriages and two children who've lived bad lives. She is not free, she feels guilt that she has messed up. Now that she's split with her partner she has more confidence in herself and is making her own decisions. Before she wouldn't want me around if he was there.
>
> My dad phones me when he wants to talk, when things are going wrong for him. But if I phone him he doesn't always want to know what's happening with me. He tries to blame me for what happened when I was a kid. He says I nearly got him put in prison. I just wish he'd admit the truth and then we could move on.

Alice is no longer in therapy. She found it useful, but her therapist moved and Alice did not want to re-establish a new therapeutic relationship. However, she continues to find her probation officer empathetic.

> She really seems to understand how I feel, although she hasn't had these sort of experiences.

Alice also finds comfort and support in Cara and the other women she met at CAST. CAST and Women And Health also provided practical help.

Coming out of prison, building a new life, is not easy and it is not made easy by the society we live in. Courses at CAST really help. There's 'Seeking Employment' which is about dealing with CVs, interviews et cetera. And the 'Self Defence' course was good for building confidence. Women drug themselves and abuse themselves. They put themselves down and feel they deserve no better. Women And Health is another useful project. Its facilities, like aromatherapy, are available at a reduced rate for claimants. They have a library of relevant books, to learn about yourself as a woman. Self-awareness is necessary. Women need to talk to discover who they are, to discover the self. It's funny prison is all women, but there's no feminism, no building up of women's self-esteem, no space to be women.

APPENDIX 4
WOMEN, CRIME AND IMPRISONMENT: OFFICIAL STATISTICS

Table 1 Offenders found guilty at all courts, by sex and type of offence, in 1989

Type of offence	Males		Females	
	No. in thousands	*Percentage*	*No. in thousands*	*Percentage*
Indictable offences				
Violence against the person	51.2	17	4.4	10
Sexual offences	7.2	2.5	0.1	0.2
Burglary	42	14	1.3	3
Robbery	4.4	1.5	0.2	0.5
Theft and handling stolen goods	107.9	37	26.6	62
Fraud and forgery	17.6	6	4.7	11
Criminal damage	8.7	3	0.7	2
Drug offences	20.2	7	2.4	6
Other (excluding motoring offences)	23.6	8	2.1	5
Motoring offences	10.8	4	0.4	1
Total	293.6	100	43	100.7

Table 1 Continued

Type of offence	Males		Females	
	No. in thousands	Percentage	No. in thousands	Percentage
Summary offences				
Offences (excluding motoring)	348.2	35	120.4	67
Motoring offences	648	65	58.9	33
Total	996.2	100	179.2	100
All offences	1289.8		222.2	

Source: Home Office (1990a: 107)

Table 2 Females aged 21 and over sentenced to immediate imprisonment at magistrates' courts for indictable offences by offence group, in 1989

Type of offence	Number sentenced	Percentage of total females sentenced	Average length in months of sentence for principal offence
Violence against the person	36	7	3.0
Sexual offences	–	–	–
Burglary	23	5	3.3
Theft and handling stolen goods	331	65	2.4
Fraud and forgery	64	12	2.7
Criminal damage	19	4	2.4
Drug offences	20	4	2.5
Motoring offences	–	–	–
Other	20	4	1.2
Total	513	101	

Source: Home Office (1990a: 172)

Table 3 Females aged 21 and over sentenced to immediate imprisonment at Crown Court for indictable offences by offence group, in 1989

Type of offence	Number sentenced	Percentage of total females sentenced	Average length in months of sentence for principal offence
Violence against the person	169	11	17.7
Sexual offences	21	1	32.0
Burglary	69	5	16.1
Robbery	40	3	29.1
Theft and handling stolen goods	561	37	8.1
Fraud and forgery	205	14	12.7
Criminal damage	32	2	24.6
Drugs offences	352	23	38.6
Motoring offences	2	0.1	4.5
Other	53	4	9.8
Total	1504	100.1	

Source: Home Office (1990a: 172)

Table 4 Persons aged 21 and over (whose records were known) in prison service establishments under sentence by number of previous convictions (all offences) (England and Wales), 30 June 1989

	All adults where previous convictions were recorded	Number of previous convictions				
		0	1–2	3–5	6–10	11+
Male						
number	21123	1925	2210	3393	5698	7897
percentage		9.1	10.5	16.0	27.0	37.4
Female						
number	604	181	115	124	90	94
percentage		30.0	19.0	20.5	14.9	15.6
All offenders						
number	21727	2106	2325	3517	5788	7991
percentage		9.7	10.7	16.2	26.6	36.8

Source: Women's National Commission (1991: 54)

Table 5 Persons aged 21 and over (whose records were known) in prison service custody under sentence for whom no previous convictions were recorded by offence (England and Wales), 30 June 1989

	Males			Females		
	Number for whom data available	*No previous convictions*		*Number for whom data available*	*No previous convictions*	
		No.	*%*		*No.*	*%*
Violence against the person	5378	539	28.0	105	38	21.0
Rape and other sexual offences	1918	278	14.4	11	5	2.8
Burglary	3975	88	4.6	34	1	0.5
Robbery	2559	126	6.5	35	3	1.6
Theft, handling, fraud and forgery	2797	204	10.6	149	19	10.5
Drugs offences	1833	477	24.8	177	85	47.0
Other offences	2137	159	8.3	75	26	14.4
Offence not recorded	518	48	2.5	18	4	2.2
Courts martial	8	6	0.3	–	–	–
All offences	21123	1925	100	604	181	100

Source: Women's National Commission (1991: 55)

* Mother and Baby Unit
† Young Offender Institution

Figure 1   Women's prisons in England and Wales

USEFUL ADDRESSES

WIP	Women In Prison 22 Highbury Grove London N5 2EA Tel: (071) 226 5879 Fax: (071) 226 1850
WISH	Women in Special Hospitals 25 Horsell Road London N5 1XL (071) 700 6684
WPRC	Women Prisoners Resource Centre Room 1 Thorpe Close Ladbroke Grove London W10 5XL (081) 968 3121
CAST	Creative And Supportive Trust 37–39 King's Terrace London NW1 0JR (071) 383 5228
BFPS	Black Female Prisoners Scheme Brixton Enterprise Centre 444 Brixton Road London SW9 (071) 733 5520

FPWP   Female Prisoners Welfare Project
                22 Highbury Grove
                London N5 2EA
                (071) 226 7727

                Akina Mama Wa Afrika
                4 Wild Court
                London WC2B 5AU
                (071) 405 0678

APS   African Prisoners Scheme
                1st Floor
                Print House
                18 Ashwin Street
                London E8
                (071) 275 9540

REFERENCES

Althusser, L. (1971) *Lenin and Philosophy and Other Essays*, London, New Left Books.

Ashworth, A. (1989) *Custody Reconsidered*, London, Centre for Policy Studies.

Austerberry, H. and Watson, S. (1983) *Women on the Margins*, London, City University, Housing Research Group.

Becker, S. (ed.) (1991) 'Introduction: from enterprise to opportunity' in *Windows of Opportunity: Public Policy and the Poor*, London, CPAG.

Benn, M. and Tchaikovsky, C. (1987) 'Dangers of being a woman', *The Abolitionist* (23).

Callender, C. (1987) 'Redundancy, unemployment and poverty' in C. Glendinning and J. Millar (eds) *Women and Poverty in Britain*, Brighton, Wheatsheaf.

Carlen, P. (1983) *Women's Imprisonment: A Study in Social Control*, London, Routledge & Kegan Paul.

Carlen, P. (1987) 'Out of care, in to custody: dimensions and deconstructions of the state's regulation of twenty-two young working-class women' in P. Carlen and A. Worrall (eds) *Gender, Crime and Justice*, Milton Keynes, Open University Press.

Carlen, P. (1988) *Women, Crime and Poverty*, Milton Keynes, Open University Press.

Carlen, P. (1990) *Alternatives to Women's Imprisonment*, Milton Keynes, Open University Press.

Carlen, P. and Tchaikovsky, C. (1985) 'Women in Prison' in P. Carlen *et al.* *Criminal Women*, Cambridge, Polity.

Carlen, P., Hicks, J., O'Dwyer, J., Christina, D. and Tchaikovsky, C. (1985) *Criminal Women*, Cambridge, Polity.

Carlen, P. and Worrall, A. (eds) (1987) *Gender, Crime and Justice*, Milton Keynes, Open University Press.

CAST (1991) *Review of CAST's Strategy: November 1990–November 1991*, London, Creative and Supportive Trust.

Connell, R. W. (1987) *Gender and Power*, Cambridge, Polity Press.

Cook, A. and Kirk, G. (1983) *Greenham Women Everywhere*, London, Pluto Press.

Department of Education and Science/Employment Department Group (1991) *Education and Training for the 21st Century*, London, HMSO.

Dobash, R. P., Dobash, R. E. and Gutteridge, S. (1986) *The Imprisonment of Women*, Oxford, Blackwell.

Donzelot, J. (1979) *The Policing of Families*, London, Hutchinson.

Eaton, M. (1986) *Justice for Women? Family, Court and Social Control*, Milton Keynes, Open University Press.

Evans, B. (1991) 'Lock up your daughters, mothers and sisters', *Observer* 15 September.

Foucault, M. (1991) *Discipline and Punish: The Birth of the Prison*, London, Penguin (first published 1975).

Gelsthorpe, L. and Morris, A. (eds) (1990) *Feminist Perspectives in Criminology*, Milton Keynes, Open University Press.

Genders, E. and Player, E. (1987) 'Women in prison: the treatment, the control and the experience' in P. Carlen and A. Worrall (eds) *Gender, Crime and Justice*, Milton Keynes, Open University Press.

Gilligan, C. (1982) *In a Different Voice*, Cambridge, Mass, Harvard University Press.

Glendinning, C. and Millar, J. (eds) (1987) *Women and Poverty in Britain*, Brighton, Wheatsheaf.

Goffman, E. (1987) *Asylums*, London, Penguin.

Grint, K. (1991) *Gender, Patriarchy and Trade Unions*, Cambridge, Polity.

Heidensohn, F. (1985) *Women and Crime*, London, Macmillan.

Hicks, J. and Carlen, P. (1985) 'Jenny: in a criminal business' in P. Carlen *et al.*, *Criminal Women*, Cambridge, Polity.

HM Inspectorate of Probation (1991) *Report on Women Offenders and Probation Service Provision*, London, Home Office.

HM Prison Service (Home Office) (1992) *Regimes for Women*, London, HMSO.

Home Office (1990a) *Criminal Statistics England and Wales 1989*, London, HMSO.

Home Office (1990b) *Prison Statistics England and Wales 1989*, London, HMSO.

Home Office (1990c) *Report on the Work of the Prison Service April 1989–March 1990*, Cm 1302, London, HMSO.

Home Office (1991) *Custody, Care and Justice: The Way Ahead for the Prison Service in England and Wales*, Cm1647, London, HMSO.

Home Office and DHSS (1975) *Report of the Committee on Mentally Abnormal Offenders*, Cm6244, London, HMSO.

Hull, C. and Coben, D. (1991) 'The survival of the fittest? The professionalism of adult education', *Adults Learning* 3(1) September.

Ignatieff, M. (1989) *A Just Measure Of Pain: The Penitentiary in the Industrial Revolution 1750–1850*, London, Penguin.

Kruttschnitt, C. (1982) 'Women, crime and dependency', *Criminology* 9(4), 495–513.

Liebling, A. (1991) 'Where are the women in Woolf?', *Prison Report* (15).

Lister, R. (1990) 'Women, economic dependency and citizenship', *Journal of Social Policy* 19(4).

Mandaraka-Sheppard, A. (1986) *The Dynamics of Aggression in Women's Prisons in England*, London, Gower.

Marshall, R. (1972) *Families Receiving Supplementary Benefit*, London, HMSO.

Matthews, R. (1991) 'Hope, health and happiness', *Criminal Justice Matters* (5) Winter.

Millar, J. (1987) 'Lone mothers' in C. Glendinning and J. Millar (eds) *Women and Poverty in Britain*, Brighton, Wheatsheaf.

Millar, J. and Glendinning, C. (1987) 'Invisible women, invisible poverty' in C. Glendinning and J. Millar (eds) *Women and Poverty in Britain*, Brighton, Wheatsheaf.

Millar, J. (1991) 'Bearing the cost' in S. Becker, (ed.) *Windows of Opportunity: Public Policy and the Poor*, London, CPAG.

Morris, A. and Wilkinson, C. (eds) (1988) *Women and the Penal System*, Cambridge, Institute of Criminology, University of Cambridge.

NACRO (1986) *Women and the Prison Medical Service*, NACRO Briefing (November), London, NACRO.

NACRO (1988) *Mothers and Babies in Prison*, NACRO Briefing (March), London, NACRO.

NACRO (1991a) *Annual Report 1990–1991*, London, NACRO.

NACRO (1991b) *The Criminal Justice Act: An Assessment by NACRO of the Act in its Final Form*, NACRO Briefing (July), London, NACRO.

NACRO National Policy Committee on Resettlement (1992) *The Resettlement Needs of Women and the Lessons of NACRO's Women Prisoners' Resource Centre*, London, NACRO.

O'Dwyer, J. and Carlen, P. (1985) 'Josie: surviving Holloway . . . and other women's prisons' in P. Carlen, *et al.*, *Criminal Women*, Cambridge, Polity.

O'Dwyer, J., Wilson, J. and Carlen, P. (1987) 'Women's imprisonment in England, Wales and Scotland: recurring issues' in P. Carlen and A. Worrall (eds) *Gender, Crime and Justice*, Milton Keynes, Open University Press.

Padel, U. and Stevenson, P. (1988) *Insiders: Women's Experience of Prison*, London, Virago.

Payne, J. (1991) 'Adult education in Inner London: a research report', *Adults Learning* 3(1) September.

Payne, S. (1991) *Women, Health and Poverty: An Introduction*, Hemel Hempstead, Harvester Wheatsheaf.

Peckham, A. (1985) *A Woman in Custody*, London, Fontana.

Posen, I. (1988) 'The female prison population' in A. Morris, and C. Wilkinson (eds) *Women and the Penal System*, Cambridge, Institute of Criminology, University of Cambridge.

Sampson, A. (1991) 'Woolf's watchwords: security, control and justice', *Prison Report* (15).

Sim, J. (1990) *Medical Power In Prisons: The Prison Medical Service in England 1774–1989*, Milton Keynes, Open University Press.

Stevenson, P. (1989) 'Women in special hospitals', *Open Mind* (41) October, 14–16.

Sumner, C. (1990) 'Foucault, gender and the censure of deviance' in L. Gelsthorpe, and A. Morris, (eds) *Feminist Perspectives in Criminology* Milton Keynes, Open University Press.

Tchaikovsky, C. (1986) 'Who guards The guards?', *The Abolitionist* (22).

Tchaikovsky, C. (1991a) 'Tattoos', *Criminal Justice Matters* (5) Winter.

Tchaikovsky, C. (1991b) 'Mixed prisons: misogynistic and misguided', *Prison Report* (16).

Thane, P. (1982) *The Foundations of the Welfare State*, London, Longman.

Townsend, S. (1989) *Mr Bevan's Dream: Why Britain Needs Its Welfare State*, London, Chatto.

Treverton-Jones, G. D. (1989) *Imprisonment: The Legal Status and Rights of Prisoners*, London, Sweet and Maxwell.

Walby, S. (1990) *Theorizing Patriarchy*, Oxford, Blackwells.

Wilkinson, C. (1988) 'The post-release experience of female prisoners' in A. Morris, and C. Wilkinson (eds) *Women and the Penal System*, Cambridge Institute of Criminology, University of Cambridge.

Wilson, E. (1977) *Women and the Welfare State*, London, Tavistock.

Women in Prison (1987) *Information Pack*, London, Women in Prison.

Women's Equality Group/London Strategic Policy Unit (1987) *Breaking the Silence*, London, Greater London Council.

Women's National Commission (1991) *Women and Prison*, London, The Women's National Commission.

Woolf L.J. and Tumim J. (1991) *Prison Disturbances April 1990*, Cm1456, London, HMSO.

INDEX